On The Silence of the Declaration of Independence

On the Silence of the Declaration of Independence

Paul Eidelberg

University of Massachusetts Press
Amherst   1976

Copyright © 1976 by
Paul Eidelberg
All rights reserved
Library of Congress Catalog Card Number 76-8759
ISBN 0-87023-216-9
Printed in the United States of America
Designed by Mary Mendell

Cataloging in Publication data appear on the
last printed page of the book.

Contents

Acknowledgments

Preface   ix

1. On Reason and Civility   1

2. On Human Dignity and Honor   17

3. The Declaration Applied: Relativism Versus Universalism   27

4. On Force and Revolution   53

5. On Equality and Self-Determination   73

Appendix   The Declaration of Independence   107

Notes   113

Acknowledgments

On the Silence of the Declaration of Independence is the first of a two-volume work on the foundations of American and Soviet foreign policy. Like its sequel, *Beyond Détente*, it was written under the auspices of the Henry Salvatori Center at Claremont Men's College. I am grateful to the Center and to the College for making this work possible.

I also wish to thank my friends William Morrisey and Donald Maletz for their perceptive and helpful criticism of the manuscript. To my wife, Phyllis, who typed the manuscript, my profound gratitude.

Claremont, 1976

Preface

I am much mistaken if the time is not just at hand when there shall be greater need than ever in America for the most accurate discussion of the principles of society . . . and the policy of states. | John Witherspoon, April, 1775

THE American people are celebrating the bicentennial of the Declaration of Independence; but are they in fact honoring the principles of that document, the principles of the American Revolution? Do they understand them? Do our statesmen?

Studies reveal that a shockingly large number of Americans do not even recognize the Declaration of Independence. Asked to comment on passages abstracted from the document, many express hostility to its fundamental principles, regarding them as subversive or suggestive of the teachings of Communism. The fact that there are so many benighted American citizens is a sorry reflection on our institutions of learning. It would be a grave error to attribute this failure of education simply to our primary and secondary schools, whose curriculums, after all, are designed by graduates of our colleges and universities: it appears that many of the learned also have an inadequate understanding of the Declaration.

Whether the American people really understand the Declaration, they do hold it in high regard. Perhaps no American document, not even the Constitution, commands so much respect. When Lincoln began the Gettysburg Address with "Four score and seven years ago," he fixed the birth of the Republic with its Declaration of Independence. And well he might. The Declaration provided the rallying call and justification of the American Revolution. Its preamble—in some cases the entire document—was adopted as the preamble of eight of the original state constitutions, signifying that the governments of those states were based on the principles and dedicated to the purposes of the Declaration. (Its appeal has been so universal that Ho Chi Minh adopted it as the model for the Vietnamese Declaration of Independence in 1945.) The Declaration may thus be regarded as the political testament of the American people, their "ancient faith." But is the political faith of citizens and statesmen today the same as that which animated the statesmen of '76?

Many statesmen since then have distilled the Declaration into a single principle: *faith in the people*, which, presumably, they found in the statement that "Governments are instituted among Men, deriving their just powers from the consent of the governed." But who are "the people"? Woodrow Wilson identified the people with the "common man." Hence, the Declaration is often understood as inaugurating and justifying the rule of the common man. But what kind of man is the common man? Is he a public-spirited and well-informed citizen, or is he so wholly preoccupied with immediate and transient interests that he mistakes the principles of the Declaration of Independence for Communist doctrine? If uncommon men are to be ruled by common men—to be sure, they never really are—it would seem to be in the interest of the former to elevate the latter.

Of course, the rule of the common man can only be justified if "all men," as the Declaration proclaims, "are created equal." But what is the meaning of this equality? The Civil War was fought largely over that question. Is equality a levelling or an elevating principle? Whatever its meaning, equality has been the dominant principle of twentieth-century American life: we are certainly more equal than ever before (as the quota system indicates).

But as a people are we happier? The Declaration emphasizes happiness, at least the unalienable right to "the pursuit of happiness." But what does this happiness consist in? Is one man's view of happiness as valid as another's? Is this the meaning or consequence of equality? If so, it would shed some light on the meaning of liberty, the unalienable right to which is also proclaimed by the Declaration. If one man's view of happiness is as justifiable as another's, then it would seem that liberty means "living as one likes," or, as some would say, liberty is self-determination.

But what is a self? Is it more than an ensemble of private thoughts and passions? Behavioral scientists deny the very notion of the self. The prevalent doctrine among contemporary social scientists is *sociological* determination, not the *self*-determination which is traceable to the Declaration of *Independence.* Yet this nation fought a war in Vietnam largely over the principle of self-determination, a war which so divided the American people as to shatter their "ancient faith." Many called that war unjust, but according to what standard of justice? Is this standard to be found in the Declaration of Independence, which speaks of the "Laws of Nature and of Nature's God"? If so, what bearing would this have on questions raised earlier, such as, Is one man's view of happiness (or justice) as valid as another's? Or does liberty mean "living as one likes"?

The statesmen of the Declaration did indeed appeal to the laws of nature and of nature's God over laws passed by a House of Commons. And because they believed in the universal truth and obligatory character of those higher laws, they pledged to the support of the Declaration and to each other not only their lives and fortunes, but their "sacred Honor." But what does "honor" mean? And is it compatible with the unqualified rule of the common man? Stated another way, is honor a democratic concept? This raises the further question, Is the Declaration a democratic document?

To answer this last question we first have to know, What is a democracy? Many would say it is the rule of the people, which reduces itself to the will of the majority. But what is the majority? Is it the majority of the people now living, or is it the majority of the electorate or of the voters? Most political scientists consider the rule of the majority to be a myth because they see no majority sharing the same opinions or interests. And if there were such a majority, they say, the result would often be tyranny. Instead, they contend that the majority changes constantly and in fact consists for the most part of a welter of groups with divergent aims and interests, groups which coalesce for electoral and legislative purposes. This, roughly, is the "pluralist" or "polyarchic" view of democracy. But what, in this view, constitutes the moral bonds of a democratic society? Many intellectuals claim that a democratic society does not require any substantive moral bonds. All that is necessary, they say, is an "agreement to disagree," in other words, mutual tolerance. Still, tolerance alone does not produce legislation. Nor does it ensure sound public policies. For the pluralist, however, there is no "public," only a multiplicity of "publics"; legislation is simply a process of bargaining between these publics—in short, a form of brokerage. Clearly, political thought has come a long way from faith in the people—and perhaps a much longer way from the statesmen of the Declaration of Independence.

Whether those statesmen had faith in the people may be left open, but one thing is certain: they believed that the success of the experiment which they inaugurated, the experiment of government by the consent of the governed, ultimately depended on an enlightened body of citizens whose participation in politics at various levels of government was to enhance their enlightenment. This is not the view of the present day "elitist" theory of democracy. Proponents of this theory contend that the successful working of democratic government requires a large apathetic mass whose wants or needs can best be served by various "elites," whether in business, in the professions, or in government.

Now, if the "pluralist" and "elitist" theories of democracy

describe, more or less, contemporary American society—for the two theories are in many respects complementary—then the celebration of the Declaration's bicentennial is a solemn mockery. And if they have more or less dominated the teaching of political science in this country, then we ought not be shocked by the existence of those benighted Americans who seem never to have studied the Declaration, or who deem its principles subversive. Given the prevalence of those two theories, the Declaration appears to be passé. Why then recur to the obsolete wisdom of the statesmen of the Declaration? Would not silence rather than celebration be more seemly?

And yet, we sense the greatness of those statesmen despite the doctrines which dominate contemporary political science. And we wonder: Are the colleges and universities of the twentieth century less capable than those of the eighteenth of producing enlightened if not architectonic statesmen? Perhaps higher education today is fundamentally defective: perhaps it is too much concerned with the training of specialists who, notwithstanding their importance, cannot take the place of men of intellectual breadth and moral vision. Sensing the difference between the statesmen of '76 and the political leaders of our own time, we are not quite confident in the rule of the new elites. Many so-called elites deify or serve merely what is common. Others disdain the common without serving what is noble. Meanwhile, the decline of statesmanship and public oratory, of professional and academic standards, proceeds apace. Throughout the liberal-conservative spectrum, on the "left" as well as on the "right," we hear the monotonous "power to the people." Such demagoguery is not absent from the academy. All the more difficult will it be, therefore, to raise up a new generation of statesmen with the courage to declare their independence from the dogmas of contemporary politics, both liberal and conservative, which have so long stultified the mentality of the American people. It is for such statesmen that I write this essay.

Transcending those stale dogmas, the Declaration is and shall always remain a radical document—radical because it goes to the roots of things. And because mankind is ever in need of being reminded of its roots, the Declaration is and shall ever remain a revolutionary document, inexhaustible in its possibilities.

Bearing these thoughts in mind, the reader should not associate me with any prevailing school, though, of course, I have had my teachers. Here I need mention only Alfred North Whitehead, whose philosophy of creativity has contributed much to my recent work, *A Discourse on Statesmanship*, the principles of which I apply in the present essay. As will soon become obvious, however, this essay makes no reference to, nor does it depend upon, any other works on the Declaration. No doubt I shall be roundly condemned by scholars for such unscholarly behavior. I am fully aware of prevailing interpretations; but whether the Declaration is a Lockean document, a product of the English Whig tradition, or whether it signals the emergence of capitalism is simply irrelevant to my purposes. The Declaration of Independence has more than historic interest, the primary concern of scholars. And, as will be shown, so far are we removed from the animating spirit of that revolutionary document that its ultimate significance cannot be brought home to us by scholarship alone. More than ever, the Declaration needs to be revitalized, to be endowed with the urgency, the relevance, and even the novelty it possessed for the revolutionaries of 1776. Accordingly, this book is more than an "interpretation" of a historical document. It seeks to elucidate, by examining what the document says, what its authors did·not and could not say, but what they somehow manifest when engaged in a dialogue intended to reveal the Declaration's "silent teachings." These teachings will be applied to the concerns of our own time.

Stated another way, the major purpose of this study is to incorporate the underlying principles of the Declaration

into a new philosophical framework that will enable thought-
ful citizens and statesmen to use those principles as criteria
for analyzing and evaluating contemporary political thought
and practice. The articulation of such criteria is made
possible by certain hitherto unexamined strata of the
Declaration. These strata—and now I touch upon the central
thesis of this inquiry—embody various aristocratic ideas and
values which must be revitalized. Indeed, the future of this
country depends on the ability of statesmen to relate the
depths to the surface of the Declaration, its aristocratic to
its democratic elements, and to translate the resulting
synthesis into public policy.

It will not be improper to mention, therefore, that this
study provides the philosophical foundation for a larger
work, *Beyond Détente*, which includes a presidential State
of the World Message based on principles drawn from the
Declaration and amplified by Washington's Farewell Address.
Assimilated to a philosophy of human nature, these principles are used to develop a new American foreign policy,
one that transcends the "moralist" as well as the "realist"
or "pragmatist" schools of international relations. (Antici-
pations of this new policy will be found in chapters 3-5 of
the present work.)

Finally, I should point out that this is the third volume
of a trilogy devoted primarily to the founding of the American Republic. Its purpose is to provide a new understanding
of American political history and, at the same time, to
generate a new school of statesmanship that will synthesize
classical and modern political science.* This synthesis,
which I have elsewhere designated "the politics of magnanimity," has guided my thoughts on the silence of the
Declaration of Independence.

---

*See my *Discourse on Statesmanship: The Design and Transformation
of the American Polity* (Urbana: University of Illinois Press, 1974);
*The Philosophy of the American Constitution: A Reinterpretation of
the Intentions of the Founding Fathers* (New York: The Free Press,
1968); *Beyond Detente* (La Salle, Ill.: Sherwood Sugden, 1976).

The language of the past is always oracular; you will only understand it as builders of the future who know the present. | Friedrich Nietzsche

One On Reason and Civility

On this I build my hope that we have not labored in vain, and that our experiment will still prove that man can be governed by reason. |
Thomas Jefferson
You will find among them [the American people] some elegance, perhaps, but more solidity; . . . some politeness, but more civility. |
John Adams

I NTRODUCTION   According to Thomas Jefferson, the Declaration of Independence "was intended to be an expression of the American mind." The American mind, however, was influenced by a variety of traditions, classical, Christian, and modern. Hence Jefferson could say that the "authority [of the Declaration] rests . . . on the harmonizing sentiments of the day, whether expressed in conversation, in letters, printed in essays, or in the elementary books of public right, as Aristotle, Cicero, Locke, Sydney, etc."[1] In other words, the Declaration is a political synthesis of diverse principles, ancient and modern. Such a synthesis is unique.

Now the task of this book is to recapture that uniqueness. I say *recapture* because the uniqueness of the Declaration has become encrusted by tradition—in fact, by a variety of traditions, each no doubt regarding itself as the true interpretation of that great document. Inasmuch as the Declaration involves, as Jefferson clearly suggests, a political synthesis of ancient and modern thought, recapturing its uniqueness will require me to uncover or at least emphasize certain possibilities latent in the document but undeveloped by any tradition. And yet, in so doing, I would be following the statesmen of the Declaration who, vis-à-vis ancient and modern writers, engaged in selective emphasis, bringing certain thoughts into the foreground, retreating others into the background. This process is an inescapable function of reason which, according to Whitehead, "is the organ of emphasis upon novelty."[2]

Every tradition involves selective emphasis. Considered as a historical synthesis, each tradition actualizes a limited number of antecedent possibilities. Stated more generally: In any creative act, whether a work of art, a political document, or a philosophical treatise, there reside numberless possibilities, not all of which, in the nature of things, can be developed equally and simultaneously either by the originating generation or by immediately succeeding ones. Certain possibilities lie dormant, waiting to evoke, as it were, a responsive chord from a more sympathetic albeit more distant generation. This is true of the Declaration of Independence.

Up to now, tradition has developed only its democratic possibilities. These have been brought to the foreground of men's thoughts, have modulated their feelings, have governed their actions. Retreated into the background are intimations of values not democratic at all, intimations of classical and even biblical values rendered silent by democracy. To give voice to that silence is the task of this essay. Not that I would deny the importance of the surface of the Declaration, which appears democratic to almost everyone. Rather, I wish to explore primarily the deeper strata of that document for its untold possibilities. As already suggested, underlying the Declaration, and more or less taken for granted by its authors, are certain aristocratic principles whose articulation might contribute to the development of a political philosophy richer in passion and more comprehensive in thought than the democratic understanding of man and society which has so profoundly shaped the character of the American mind during the present century.

For analytical purposes, the Declaration will be divided into four parts. The first part, beginning with certain elemental truths, purposes, and organizing principles of government, and ending with the call for revolution, will be termed the "preamble." The second part, consisting of the catalog of grievances, will be called precisely that or the "accusation." The third part, referring to the colonies' repeated petitions for redress of grievances, and ending with the challenge to Britain and to mankind, will be called the "denunciation." The fourth and last part, containing the colonies' formal severance from Great Britain, will be called the "peroration."

The Declaration was not only intended to be an expression of the American mind, but, as Jefferson added, it was also intended "to give to that expression the proper tone and spirit called for by the occasion." Listen to the language of the preamble:

> When in the Course of human events, it becomes necessary for one people to dissolve the political bands which have connected them with another, and to assume among the powers of the earth, the separate and equal station to which the Laws of Nature and of Nature's God entitle them, a decent respect to the opinions of mankind requires that they should declare the causes which impel them to the separation.

Note the dignity, the lofty tone of this language. It bespeaks the civility of its authors. These are men of aristocratic temperament. Note, too, the spirit of this language, its universalism. It speaks of thought transcending time and place. These are men of philosophic temperament. Yet the language was intended to be "an expression of the American mind," expressing its "harmonizing sentiments"; and this urbane language of universality of spirit was "called for by the occasion." The occasion, of course, was a political revolution. If, therefore, the language of the Declaration was in truth called for by that revolutionary occasion, then the meaning of the Revolution must be reflected in the tone and spirit of that language. But the tone and spirit of that language speaks to us of the civility of its authors and of their philosophic temperament. To this extent the Declaration is the expression less of "the American mind" than of those who numbered among America's noblest statesmen. What entitles these men to that honor or distinction is that they sought to elevate the American mind by associating the "sentiments of the day" with thoughts transcending time and place.

The occasion did indeed require luminous and exalted thoughts. The statesmen of the Declaration knew they were precipitating a revolution of universal significance: wherefore the universalism of their language, the appeal to the laws of nature and of nature's God. To dissolve the *political* bands which connected them with Great Britain—this they could do. To dissolve the *moral* bands which connected them with their British brethren—this they could not do. For the laws of nature comprise a universal moral law ineluctably binding all mankind, in the light of which the statesmen of the Declaration could proclaim (in opposition to Lockean epistemology):

> We hold these truths to be self-evident, that all men are created equal, that they are endowed by their Creator with certain unalienable rights, that among these are Life, Liberty and the pursuit of Happiness.[3]

Before the laws of nature, before a universal moral law, all men are necessarily equal. And yet it may be misleading to speak of men "before" the laws of nature. These laws are not simply external; they are immanent in human nature. They are the very principles which distinguish the human from the sub-human. As James Wilson put it: "The law of nature is immutable, not by the effect of an arbitrary disposition, but because it has its foundation in the nature, constitution, and mutual relations of men and things." Not only was Wilson a signer of the Declaration, he was also one of the most important members of the convention that drafted the Constitution. In his law lectures, which he delivered at the University of Pennsylvania in 1790-91, Wilson called upon the authority of Cicero for his own disquisition on the law of nature:

> This law, or right reason, as Cicero calls it, is thus beautifully described by that eloquent philosopher. "It is, indeed," says he, "a true law, conformable to nature, diffused among all men, unchangeable, eternal. By its commands, it calls men to their duty: by its prohibitions, it deters them from vice. . . . Neither by the senate, nor by the people, can its powerful obligation be dissolved. . . . It is not one law at Rome, another at Athens; one law now, another hereafter: it is the same eternal and immutable law, given at all times and to all nations:* for God, who is its author and promulgator, is always the sole master and sovereign of mankind."[4]

Since the law of nature (known also as the "moral law") is "diffused among all men," all men are to that extent equal. Furthermore, precisely because that moral law is eternal and immutable, all the generations of mankind are equal. It follows that the ultimate foundation of man's unalienable rights to life, liberty, and the pursuit of happiness is not in "History," not in some eschatological epoch, nor in some privileged class or generation, but in the laws of *nature* and *of* nature's God.

And so our philosophically tempered statesmen continue by saying:

> That to secure these rights, Governments are instituted among Men, deriving their just powers from the consent of the governed,—that whenever any Form of Government becomes destructive of these ends, it is the Right of the People to alter or to abolish it. . . .

---

*This is contrary to Locke, who regarded justice or morality as conventional: "good or evil is drawn on us from the will and power of the law-maker." *An Essay Concerning Human Understanding*, II, xxviii, 5.

That government is an artifact does not mean that prior to its establishment men lived in a state of nature, devoid of moral law. Contrary to one of the fundamental principles of modern contract theory, Jefferson regarded man as a social animal. He rejected what he called "the principle of Hobbes, that justice is founded in contract solely, and does not result from the construction of man." "Man," he wrote, "was destined for society. . . . He was endowed with a sense of right and wrong . . . The moral sense, or conscience . . . is as much a part of our constitution as that of feeling, seeing, or hearing."[5] Accordingly, the contract resulting in the establishment of government (and the obligatory nature of that contract) presupposes the classical-*cum*-Christian notion that man is a social being endowed with a moral sense or conscience (a notion denied by both Locke and Hobbes). This subtle interplay of ancient and modern motifs renders more profound and comprehensible the Declaration's currently misunderstood principle that governments derive their *just* powers from the consent of the governed.* Whatever the meaning of consent, the consent of the governed is not alone sufficient to make political power just, so long as we recognize that the governed, as envisioned by the Declaration, are subject to the natural/divine law. In the eclipse of the latter, might— the power of mere numbers—would make right, and the American Revolution would be deprived of moral justification. The principle of consent is derivative. Its moral authority must be traced through deeper strata, to man's very nature as a critical being. Such a being makes a rational distinction between political power and justice. This distinction lies at the heart of the Declaration. The central question is whether certain powers or acts of government are consistent with justice (the sense of which is immanent

*The topic of consent will be discussed in Chapter 5, where it will be related to the principle of self-determination and United States foreign policy.

in human nature responding to the natural/divine law). Thus understood, that distinction enlarges the scope of political reason. In the determination of whether any form of government is just, it is not enough for rulers to derive their powers from the consent of the governed; they must also exercise those powers in consonance with the ends for which government is instituted, among which ends are life, liberty, and the pursuit of happiness.

Now it happens that the distinction between political power and justice corresponds to the distinction between the forms and ends of government. The forms are made by men: they entail laws promulgated by kings and parliaments; they call for the allegiance of a particular community. In contrast, the ends derive from nature: they comprise a body of universal moral truths obligatory upon all mankind, kings and parliaments included. Adherence to the forms represents adherence to the legal or to what is right by convention; adherence to the ends represents adherence to the just or to what is right by nature. This distinction between the legal and the just is, of course, of ancient origin. Whether exemplified in the conflict between Antigone and Creon or between Socrates and Thrasymachus, it is of revolutionary significance, for it places on trial the acts of every form of government, whether of the One, or of the Few, or of the Many, and enables the governed to judge those acts by universal standards of justice. And should government fail to conform to those standards, that is, should the legal fail to conform to the just, then the governed may withdraw their allegiance from their governors. However familiar this teaching may be, its revolutionary significance needs to be emphasized. And yet, despite its revolutionary significance, the distinction between the legal and the just does not reveal what is unique about the Declaration of Independence.

What is unique and, at the same time, revolutionary is this simple and silent assertion: Henceforth government is

to be based primarily on *rational* and not *customary* foundations. Not immemorial tradition, not the authority of
kings claiming divine sanction, but reason, God-given
reason, whose light is available *in principle* to all mankind—
this is the only legitimate foundation of government, and
*the only justification for government by the consent of the
governed.*

A remarkable Declaration. Note the confidence of its
statesmen in the power of reason. Said Jefferson: "Fix
reason firmly in her seat and call to her tribunal every fact,
every opinion."[6] Note, too, the boldness of the Declaration—identifying the American cause with the cause of
mankind, engendering, by the universalism of its principles,
the notion of America's historic purpose. Again Jefferson:

> May it [the Declaration of Independence] be to the world, what I
> believe it will be (to some part sooner, to others later, but finally
> to all), the signal of arousing men to burst the chains . . . [of]
> ignorance and superstition . . . and to assume the blessings . . .
> self-government. . . . All eyes are opened, or opening, to the
> rights of man.[7]

This confidence in reason and this notion of America's
historic purpose is reflected in that realistic work, *The
Federalist*. In *Federalist* 1 Hamilton declares:

> It has been frequently remarked that it seems to have been reserved
> to the people of this country, by their conduct and example, to
> decide the important question, whether societies of men are really
> capable or not of establishing good government from reflection and
> choice, or whether they are forever destined to depend for their
> political constitutions on accident and force.[8]

Hitherto, governments owed their origin to force and
accident (such as the accidents of birth and personality).
They lacked *rational* foundations, foundations consistent
with the laws of nature and *of* nature's God. Hence, any
government based solely on force and accident is contrary

to nature and to nature's God, contrary, say, to the peculiarly human.

To grasp the peculiarly human and to uncover thereby the philosophy of man latent in the Declaration, one must first ask, *What kind of being is man that he, unlike all other creatures, should be endowed with those unalienable rights to life, liberty, and the pursuit of happiness?* Surely a being thus endowed must be potentially capable of governing himself without impairing the unalienable rights of others. Presumably, such a being would have the capacity to distinguish between his immediate wants and his long-range interests. He would have to understand how the pursuit of his own interests may affect the well-being of others, and how the wants and interests of others may affect his own. To this end he would have to be considerate of the claims advanced by others. And if he is to show "a decent respect to the opinions of mankind," he would have to address the reason rather than the passions of mankind, which means he would have to defend his own claims by reasoning. Finally, he and his fellows would have to know how to bring into mutual adjustment their competing claims and interests if the so-called rights to life, liberty, and the pursuit of happiness are to be something more than a facade for foolishness and petty egoism.

Two qualities, then, seem to distinguish the human from the sub-human. One obviously is the discriminating and synthesizing power of reason. The other quality is more difficult to name. It is suggested by the tone and spirit of the Declaration, especially by the phrase "a decent respect to the opinions of mankind." I shall call it "civility," with the understanding that it issues from intellectual as well as moral virtues. On the one hand, it presupposes the ability to appreciate diverse points of view. On the other hand, it presupposes moderation or self-restraint, hence the power to control those passions which sometimes obscure the differences between men and brutes. But to see even more clearly the essence of civility, permit me to cite the following passage from *Federalist* 1, where Hamilton candidly admits that

> So numerous indeed and so powerful are the causes which serve to give a false bias to the judgment, that we, upon many occasions, see wise and good men on the wrong as well as on the right side of questions of the first magnitude to society. This circumstance, if duly attended to, would furnish a lesson of moderation to those who are ever so much persuaded of their being in the right in any controversy. And a further reason for caution, in this respect, might be drawn from the reflection that we are not always sure that those who advocate the truth are influenced by purer principles than their antagonists. Ambition, avarice, personal animosity, party opposition, and many other motives not more laudable than these, are apt to operate upon those who support as those who oppose the right side of a question.[9]

There is an urbane and healthy skepticism in these words discernible beneath their disarming civility, a civility which attains to nothing less than magnanimity. Their kinship with the tone, spirit, and especially the reasonableness of the Declaration is unmistakable.

In answering the question, *What kind of being is man . . .?* I have simply elaborated upon certain characteristics of the American mind suggested by Jefferson, but which I ascribed to the statesmen of the Declaration. The Declaration may therefore appear to be a species of "autobiography." Be this as it may,[10] its thought (as well as its tone and spirit) compels me to conclude that it was primarily addressed to, and intended for, the society of an enlightened race of men, men whose life, liberty, and pursuit of happiness would be informed by reason and adorned by that civility—that decent respect and moderation—which makes it unnecessary for men so frequently to clamor for their human rights. Hence the peroration of the Declaration could refer to "the *good* People of these Colonies" (italics added). Hence some thirty-seven years later, in his famous letter to Adams (28 October 1813), Jefferson could say that Americans "may safely and advantageously reserve to themselves a wholesome control over their public affairs, and a degree of freedom, which, in the hands of the canaille of the cities of Europe, would be instantly perverted to the demolition and destruction of everything public and private." These words carry us up and allow us to look down from the heights of Monticello.

In the affirmation of the power of reason and in the exemplification of that complex virtue called civility, that is, in the definition of man as *homo rationalis et civilis*, I find the key to the philosophy of man underlying the Declaration and long buried by the democratic tradition. Far from being merely a declaration of political independence, that document proclaims the very independence of the human intellect. The primacy of ancient tradition was to give way, and the primacy of living reason was henceforth to be the ruling principle of political life. Wherefore Madison could proclaim in *Federalist* 14:

> Is it not the glory of the people of America, that, whilst they have paid a decent regard to the opinions of former times and other nations, they have not suffered a blind veneration for antiquity, for custom, or for names, to overrule the suggestions of their own good sense, the knowledge of their own situation, and the lessons of their own experience?[11]

The authority of reason, however, is of universal significance. Accordingly, Madison, like Hamilton, identifies the good of America with the good of mankind. He continues:

> To this manly spirit, posterity will be indebted for the possession, and the world for the example, of the numerous innovations displayed on the American theatre, in favor of private rights and public happiness. . . . Happily for America, happily, we trust, for the whole human race, they [the leaders of the Revolution] pursued

a new and . . . noble course. They accomplished a revolution
which has no parallel in the annals of human society. They reared
the fabrics of governments which have no model on the face of the
globe.[12]

When most of the state governments incorporated the
preamble of the Declaration or its equivalent into their
constitutions, the rationality of the Declaration was given
institutional form.[13] Power was divided between legislative,
executive, and judicial branches designed to guard against
the very grievances that made it "necessary for one people
to dissolve the political bands which . . . connected them
with another." They were designed by civilized men to
place civilized restraints on men's most dangerous passions.
They were, therefore, designed to enlarge the role of reason
in political life, of "reflection and choice" rather than of
"accident and force." Thus they bear witness to the architectonic principle of the Declaration.

To be sure, the power of reason may be abused. In the
absence of civility it may become the instrument of consuming appetites and domineering passions. Was not reason
employed in the acts of the British government denounced
by the Declaration? But those acts, and therefore *that*
reason, violated the laws of nature or the natural/divine
law as apprehended by a higher or more comprehensive
mode of intellection. Accordingly, we may distinguish two
kinds or functions of reason which may sometimes conflict
with each other. One may be described as Metaphysical,
Holistic, or Teleological; the other as Pragmatic, Specialized,
or Technological. It should be understood, however, that
these two kinds or functions of reason, though distinct, are
interrelated.

The metaphysical reason is the architectonic principle of
the Declaration. It apprehends those laws of nature and of
nature's God which may be enjoyed in their contemplation,
or which may become ends motivating political action and

institutions. Also, the metaphysical reason makes possible the distinction between the legal and the just, a distinction which may generate reform or revolution. Furthermore, the metaphysical reason invisibly kindles the development of a coherent and comprehensive view of life, liberating men from a welter of immediate wants, of narrow and transient interests. This, of course, it could not do were it not for the accomplishments of the pragmatic reason whose tendency, however, is to become preoccupied with those transient wants and interests. (More often than not, it is that preoccupation which engenders political conflict as well as conflict with the prehensions of the metaphysical reason.)[14] Finally, it is preeminently the metaphysical reason that makes man the *meta*physical animal, the only animal that can transcend the physical. By virtue of that transcendence men enjoy freedom. This last point requires elaboration.

We have seen that the Declaration affirms the power of reason to apprehend universal moral standards in terms of which men may criticize the acts of government as well as the "opinions of mankind." This implies the possibility of intellectual detachment or independence, which means that our thoughts concerning justice, for example, are not wholly determined by non-rational or sociological forces. In other words, the statesmen of the Declaration affirm the possibility of moral insight, which presupposes the freedom of the intellect from external compulsion. Whereas intellectual freedom makes revolution possible, only moral insight can render revolution justifiable. Such insight reveals the disparity between the actual and the potential, between the historical and the trans-historical, by which I again mean the laws of nature and of nature's God. Inasmuch as those laws distinguish the human from the sub-human, their apprehension is fundamental for, though not unqualifiedly determinitive of, the question of how men should live and how societies should be governed.* Let us call those laws *ideals*, and let us define an ideal as an *end* entertained as an *idea*. An ideal is *a perfection to be aimed at*, a perfection which can be conceptualized or spoken of but never fully achieved. It is a lure for action, which suggests that knowledge of perfection is the precondition (if not the articulation) of human freedom. This is but to say that freedom is action consistent with insight, not mere opinion. It must be emphasized, however, that freedom presupposes the self-directed activity of the metaphysical intellect on which men's unalienable right to freedom of thought is ultimately grounded.

Although freedom involves the self-directed activity of the metaphysical intellect, that activity is limited by its aim, namely, truth. Truth, in other words, is the constraint imposed on reason and the limitation imposed on freedom. This thought is beautifully expressed in Whitehead's *Adventures of Ideas:*

> There is a freedom lying beyond circumstance, derived from the direct intuition that life can be grounded upon its absorption in what is changeless amid change. This is the freedom at which Plato was groping, the freedom which Stoics and Christians obtained as the gift of Hellenism. It is the freedom of that virtue directly derived from the source of all harmony. For it is conditioned only by its adequacy of understanding. And understanding has this quality that, however it be led up to, it issues in the soul freely conforming its nature to the supremacy of insight. It is the reconciliation of freedom with the compulsion of truth.[15]

Without the compulsion of truth—of metaphysical truth—reason is reduced to the role of instrument, the pragmatic slave of turbulent passions and interests. Freedom then dissolves into the random play of blind force and accident: men

---

*The problem of moral judgment, in contradistinction to moral principles, will be discussed in Chapter 4.

become statistics, the last vestige of equality. This is not the equality of which the Declaration speaks. In the profoundest sense, what renders all men equal is what renders them commensurate with one another, and that is truth, insight into perfection.

Two   On Human Dignity and Honor

A constitution founded on these [republican] principles introduces
knowledge among the people and inspires them with a conscious
dignity becoming freemen. | John Adams
To that honour, whose connexion with virtue is indissoluble, a
republican government produces the most unquestionable title. The
principle of virtue is allowed to be hers: if she possesses virtue, she
also possesses honour. | James Wilson

E NDOWED by nature and by nature's God with the
rights to life, liberty, and the pursuit of happiness,
man, the metaphysical animal, is the only animal
endowed with dignity. The source of that dignity, it should
be emphasized, is the metaphysical reason which transcends
the concerns of everyday life. Of this reason Whitehead has
said:

> It is not concerned with keeping alive. It seeks with disinterested
> curiosity an understanding of the world. Naught that happens is
> alien to it. It is driven forward by the ultimate faith that all par-
> ticular fact is understandable as illustrating the general principles
> of its own nature and of its status among other particular facts. It
> fulfils its function when understanding has been gained. Its sole
> satisfaction is that experience has been understood. It presupposes
> life, and seeks life rendered good with the goodness of under-
> standing. Also so long as understanding is incomplete, it remains to
> that extent unsatisfied. It thus constitutes itself the urge from the
> good life to the better life.[1]

We must agree with Whitehead that the metaphysical reason
"flickers with very feeble intensity" throughout the generality of mankind. Nevertheless, the ordinary man's admiration of, or his deference to, men of wisdom indicates the
intuition of the metaphysical reason and, therewith, the

source of human dignity. By that intuition man knows he is more than an animal.

It follows that human dignity consists of intellectual and moral excellence, and that the rights of which the Declaration speaks stand or fall with the recognition of that consistency. This conclusion can be reached another way. To complain of being treated like an animal is tacitly to acknowledge that one is a metaphysical animal. More apparent in the complaint, however, is that spirited element of the soul often associated with the feeling of indignation. This feeling is exemplified in the Declaration's catalog of grievances against King George III which concludes as follows:

> He has plundered our seas, ravaged our Coasts, burnt our towns, and destroyed the lives of our people.—He is at this time transporting large Armies of foreign Mercenaries to complete the works of death, desolation and tyranny, already begun with circumstances of Cruelty and perfidy scarcely paralleled in the most barbarous ages, and totally unworthy of the Head of a civilized nation. . . . He has . . . . endeavored to bring on the enhabitants of our frontiers, the merciless Indian Savages, whose known rule of warfare, is an undistinguished destruction of all ages, sexes and conditions.

The feeling of indignation illustrated here presupposes a feeling of self-respect, the other side of which is the exclusively human capacity to feel self-contempt. As Nietzsche so vividly put it, "Man is the beast with red cheeks," the only animal possessing a sense of shame.

The sense of shame should be thought of as a power which enables men to control their animal desires. It determines that moderation or self-restraint associated earlier with civility. Lacking the sense of shame, men do indeed become beasts—worse, barbarians with technique. On the other hand, the same sense of shame (but therefore the sense of dignity) underlies the exhortation, "Act like a man!" We ought not expect to discover one cow urging another of its species to act like a cow. In the hierarchy of nature bovine dignity does not exist.

Lest it be thought, however, that human dignity or self-respect presupposes only the existence of creatures inferior to mankind, I hasten to point out that such a conclusion ignores the phenomenon of self-contempt. Self-contempt is inconceivable without the operation of the critical intellect, which distinguishes between what is noble, what is ordinary, and what is base. The critical intellect turned against ourselves quite readily informs us that we are still animals, that even as metaphysical animals none of us is without fault or deficiency. Accordingly, man's dignity requires that, in the order of the universe, there exist not only inferior creatures beneath him, but a superior Being above him, a Being whose perfection is the lure of man's metaphysical intellect in its ceaseless quest for the highest happiness, wisdom.[2]

To that Being whom they call "the Supreme Judge of the world" the statesmen of the Declaration appeal "for the rectitude of [their] intentions." This appeal to the "Supreme Judge" in the peroration is consistent with their appeal to the "Laws of Nature's God" in the preamble. In neither case is *history* the ultimate standard by which they judge themselves or their British brethren. Their dignity depends on their refusing to bow to the chimera of history—that dodge of timid men who look upon success as the criterion of rightness. Nor do those hardy statesmen of the Declaration appeal to world opinion. To the contrary: while they show a decent respect to the opinions of mankind by declaring the causes which impel them to separate from Great Britain, they in fact deny the opinion in question. For that opinion is nothing other than the respectable opinion that identifies the just with the legal, according to which the statesmen of the Declaration would be branded traitors. Far from being governed by world opinion, these statesmen, after repeated petitions for a redress of grievances, and after appealing to the "native justice and magnanimity" of their British brethren, boldly declare: "We must, therefore, acquiesce in the necessity, which denounces [meaning, at the time, *announces*] our Separation, and hold them, as we hold the rest of Mankind, Enemies in War, in Peace Friends." Such is the language of genuine statesmen, of spirited men whose dignity or self-respect does not depend on the opinions or approval of mankind but rather on that Supreme Judge under whose sanction they conclude, saying: "And for the support of this Declaration . . . we mutually pledge to each other our Lives, our Fortunes and our sacred Honor."

Notice that they make their pledge to *each other*. This signifies that the statesmen of the Declaration pledge their honor as individuals. Somehow their dignity *qua* species, that is, as *homo rationalis et civilis*, does not exhaust their dignity *qua* individuals; it does not fully account for their sense of honor or self-respect. Self-respect may therefore be regarded as the intensification or modulation of respect for oneself *qua* species by the respect for oneself *qua* individual. This modulating power of the self renders the individual ultimately though not exclusively responsible for the manner in which he pursues happiness. I say *not exclusively* because of the internal relatedness or mutual immanence of all things. Just as each thing (or individual) differentially extends its character into the environment, so the environment (which includes all individuals) differentially enters into the character of each thing. Nevertheless, mutual immanence ought not obscure the primacy of individuality. For individuality, or the *principium individuationis*, is the primordial cause and consequence of the separation of all things, the transcendence of which requires the synthesizing power of the metaphysical reason. (Here I am merely translating into metaphysical terms the phrase "separate and equal" occurring near the outset of the Declaration.) From this ontological primacy of individuality follows the moral primacy of the individual, so that a dignity or honor is derived primarily from his individuality and secondarily from the virtues he shares with members of his own species.

Still, what does it mean to pledge one's *sacred honor?* Clearly, the word honor as used by the statesmen of the Declaration is not to be confused with prestige, which denotes reputation, and which, of course, may be based on an illusion. But let is explore, with the help of the Oxford English Dictionary, certain meanings of honor compatible with its occurrence in the Declaration.

To begin with, each signatory pledges his honor "for the support of this Declaration." By so doing he "stakes his personal title to credit and estimation on the truth of his statement." Of paramount significance here is not the relationship between honor and reputation (or prestige), but rather the dependency of the speaker's reputation on the *truth of his statement* in contradistinction to his own *truthfulness.* You may be truthful, meaning you may be honest: you may say what you believe to be true. But what you say may in fact be untrue. And if untrue, instead of being praised for your honesty you may be despised as an honest fool, perhaps even condemned as a dangerous one. In other words, honesty divorced from truth is not worthy of honor. Therein lies the reason why we do not speak of a person's sacred honesty and why we do speak of a person's sacred honor.

To say that even a fool can be honest is to admit that truthfulness does not require much thoughtfulness. The critical and synthesizing power of reason remains undeveloped in many an honest man. Nevertheless, truthfulness points beyond itself to the respect for truth. We see this respect for truth in the self-respect men derive from their own honesty. Here I am reminded of Whitehead's remark that "truthfulness as an element of one's own self-respect issues from a reverence for Reason in its own right"—hence for truth in its own right.[3] This reverence for reason and truth helps to clarify why the statesmen of the Declaration pledge to each other their *sacred* honor.

From the preceding consideration certain conclusions follow: First, the source of honor is truth and the respect for truth. Second, honor depends more on self-respect than on the respect or favorable opinion of others. Third, other things being equal, statesmen governed by honor will have a more coherent and comprehensive understanding of political affairs—will have a profounder realism—than will those governed by considerations of prestige. This last conclusion calls for elaboration, but discussion of other aspects of honor must intervene.

In the preamble of the Declaration a clear distinction is made between opinion and truth. A civilized person will show "a decent respect to the opinions of mankind." He will do this by stating his reasons for disagreeing with those opinions or for not abiding by their imperatives. And yet, by showing a decent respect to the opinions of mankind, the statesmen of the Declaration teach us something about decency itself. Decency requires not only that we justify our opposition to commonly accepted opinions, but that we regard those opinions as articulations of *thought* rather than of material *interests*. In other words, decency requires that we avoid the behavioral reduction of human thought to the level of the non-rational. (This reductionism, applied to behaviorists, calls to mind the notice at the sideshow in Swift, "The largest elephant in the world except himself to be seen here.") Furthermore, by respecting opinions as expressions of thought and not of mere interests, the statesmen of the Declaration affirm their respect for man as the truth-seeking animal. This respect for truth—from which followed the elevation of those principles proclaimed in the preamble over the opinions of mankind—is constitutive of their own self-respect. Viewed in this light, to pledge one's sacred honor is to affirm, in a most emphatic way, allegiance to one's publicly proclaimed moral principles. It is to give assurance of wholehearted dedication to one's cause. This wholeheartedness would be lacking were it not for belief in the universal truth and justice of one's cause. Such wholehearted dedication—which involves the will and determination to undertake (and *persevere* in) a struggle involving the danger of violent death—is not to be expected from skeptics or from a nation of moral relativists. In contrast, the statesmen of the Declaration firmly believed in the universal validity of the principles enunciated in the preamble. Because the "repeated injuries and usurpations" described in the accusation denied those principles, the statesmen could pledge their lives, fortunes, and scared honor with logical and moral consistency, and, moreover, they could be expected to persevere in the struggle for American independence.

So here we behold the two cardinal consequences of honor, that is, of honor rooted in truth. On the one hand, honor enlarges the intellect, on the other hand, honor fortifies the will. And yet, the mere fact that the statesmen of the Declaration pledge their honor is indicative of the unpleasant fact that the multitude would seldom stake their lives and fortunes on behalf of a just cause were it not for the promptings of the few. "We ought not to forget," wrote John Stuart Mill,

> that there is an incessant and ever-flowing current of human affairs towards the worse, consisting of all the follies, all the vices, all the negligences, indolences, and supineness of mankind, which is only controlled, and kept from sweeping all before it, by the exertions which some persons constantly, and others by fits, put forth in the direction of good and worthy objects.[4]

Because men are too often ruled by the impulse of passion, the far-seeing statesmen of the Revolution warn that "Prudence, indeed, will dictate that Governments long established should not be changed for light and transient causes." Conversely, because "mankind are more disposed to suffer, while evils are sufferable, than to right themselves by abolishing the forms to which they are accustomed," these otherwise moderate statesmen hasten to add: "But when a long train of abuses and usurpation, pursuing invariably the same Object evinces a design to reduce them under absolute Despotism; it is their right, it is their duty, to throw off such Government." And so the many—and they include men from all walks of life—have to be called to duty by the few, the men of honor. Here duty and honor are not coterminous. Both require us to act justly. But honor reaches out beyond the just to the noble. Men may rightly be required to fulfill their duties. They can hardly be required to act nobly.

At this point I must return to and elaborate upon the conclusion that honor rooted in truth enlarges the intellect, or that statesmen governed by honor are more apt to possess a more coherent and comprehensive understanding of political affairs than is to be expected from those governed by prestige.

According to the eighteenth-century lexicon, "honor [is] distinct from mere probity, and . . . supposes in a gentleman a stronger abhorrence of perfidy, falsehood, or cowardice, and a more elevated and delicate sense of virtue, than are usually found in [ordinary decent men]." Now a statesman animated by honor will certainly be concerned about the effects of his actions upon others. This concern motivates inquiry and reflection. In deliberating on public matters, such a statesman will weigh alternative public policies, will consider their long-range as well as immediate consequences. This means that, prior to reaching political decisions, he will take account of the different kinds of men composing his community, their diverse opinions, passions, and interests, their virtues and their vices. Such considerations cannot but enlarge his intellect. Still, we are only at the surface of the matter.

To say that a statesman animated by honor is guided

more by abiding truths than by transient opinions is almost to say that his political thought owes much to reflection on the political wisdom of the past. (Recall Jefferson's reference to Aristotle and Cicero, as well as to Locke and Sidney.) Also, unlike the political pragmatist preoccupied with the immediate and with immediate results—the base path to popularity and prestige—the statesman who ventures on the more difficult path of honor and glory will be concerned about posterity's enjoyment of liberty and happiness. If he is to be celebrated by distant generations, his political thought must be both original and of universal significance. To paraphrase an earlier reference to Madison: Is it not the glory of the statesmen who founded this nation that, whilst they paid a decent regard to the wisdom of former times, they have not suffered a blind veneration for antiquity to overrule the dictates of their own experience and judgment? To these statesmen, posterity will be indebted for the possession, and the world for the example, of novel ideas and institutions favorable to personal liberty and public happiness. Finally, the political thought of statesmen concerned with honor rather than with mere popularity will be addressed primarily to men like themselves, who alone could appreciate and preserve their originality and universal significance. Surely these would be philosophic statesmen, men who possess a coherent and comprehensive understanding of political life.

Infinitely more than the political pragmatist, the statesman brings philosophy to bear on action, applies theory to practice. Why? Because the overflowing energy of his soul, the thrust of his individuality, seeks to extend itself through space and time. And this energy would be dissipated were it not for the creative agency of reason whose primary function "is to constitute, emphasize, and criticize the final causes and strength of aims directed towards them."[5] This is precisely the task of political philosophy, yet it finds exemplification in the Declaration of Independence whose

statesmen were attuned to the works of political philosophers. They were not content to remain the subjects of a
government whose purposes did not coincide with their
own. In their own minds these statesmen possessed more
elevated standards of what ought to be the ends of political
life and of the manner in which those ends should be pursued. Their standards constituted a criticism of "political
reality." But the meaning of that political reality was
reconstituted by those same standards. Thus, when the
statesmen of the Declaration say "let Facts be submitted to
a candid world" and then proceed to enumerate various acts
of the British government, these acts would not have been
deemed unjust, would not have been resented and vigorously resisted, were it not for the standards of those
statesmen, especially their sense of honor. Indeed, those
"facts" would not have been selected for emphasis, hence
would have had no *actual* meaning, were it not for the
values of these statesmen or for the political philosophy
adumbrated in the preamble. The entire catalog of grievances,
echoing the proposition that all men are created equal, may
be summarized as follows: You have treated us like brutes,
as if we were an inferior species. But by God we are rational
beings, equally endowed with the rights to life, liberty, and
the pursuit of happiness![6]

Three The Declaration Applied: Relativism versus Universalism

I do not think it is permissible to draw lines between the "good" and the "bad" and be true to the constitutional mandate to let all ideas alone. . . . Government does not sit to reveal where the "truth" is. | Justice William O. Douglas
How do you describe the war of 1776? Was that a war of national liberation, or wasn't it? | Senator J. William Fulbright (Hearings on Vietnam—1966)
Recognizing that the quest for useful knowledge transcends the differences between ideologies and social systems, we have agreed to expand United States and Soviet co-operation in many areas of science and technology. | President Richard M. Nixon
It would be hard to identify the exact source of that inner intuition . . . which prompted our refusal to enter the NKVD schools. . . . Our decision even ran counter to our material interests. . . . Without even knowing it ourselves, we were ransomed by the small change in copper that was left from the golden coins our great-grandfathers had expended, at a time when morality was not considered relative and when the distinction between good and evil was very simply perceived by the heart. | Alexander Solzhenitsyn

A S intimated above, the major purpose of this chapter is to examine certain aspects of contemporary political thought and practice from the perspective of the Declaration of Independence. The chapter is divided into three parts. Part I explores the roots of moral relativism, a doctrine which has significantly altered the mentality of American statesmen, causing them, if not to abandon, then to adhere only half-heartedly to, the universalistic principles of the Declaration. Part II reveals how moral relativism actually affects the formulation and conduct of American foreign policy and how it is undermining the future of the

United States as a free and independent Republic. Part III contrasts relativism with the universalism of the Declaration, showing wherein the latter avoids dogmatism or doctrinairism and conduces to a politics of magnanimity.

I

The Declaration of Independence is a call to arms in a cause charged with death and destruction. Still, a "decent respect to the opinions of mankind" required the statesmen of the Declaration to justify what world opinion then deemed an act of treason, namely, the Americans' refusal to obey the laws of parliament and king. For at the time in question, most men identified the legal with the just, holding the not unreasonable opinion that to be just is to be law-abiding. Inasmuch, however, as the laws may be enacted by the One, or the Few, or the Many, and in their own interest rather than for the sake of the common good, there will exist as many notions of justice as there are regimes or distinct forms of government. Mankind could thus be splintered into a multiplicity of distinct species, each with its own morality or way of life, and none would recognize any universal moral standard by which to judge whether one species' way of life was preferable to another's. Under such a dispensation, "justice" would consist in the will of the stronger. Might would make right. We are back to Plato's *Republic*, yet very much in the pages of the twentieth century.

When Thrasymachus defined *justice* as "the interest of the stronger," he was stating, incautiously but candidly, the doctrine of legal realism or positivism which has long dominated American law schools.* Were the proponents of this doctrine consistent, as well as "just," they would always abet the interests of the "stronger." But then, not unlike Thrasymachus, their self-respect, indeed their very

*That many if not most lawyers may nonetheless be openly moralistic is a matter tacitly explained, in part, below, pp. 32-33.

respect for reason, rescues them from an absurd logic: They discover that the "stronger" may not always know his own interests. Be this as it may, inasmuch as the stronger may be the One, or the Few, or the Many, the rejection of the distinction between the legal and the just in effect dignifies all forms of regimes including tyrannies such as Nazi Germany and the Soviet Union—and justifies the conquests they make as well. This is precisely the practical consequence of the various forms of relativism which have ruled higher education in the United States, especially during the last four decades, and which now permeate even the mentality of the ordinary citizen. Except for Marxism (itself a subtle form of relativism), no prevailing doctrine is more opposed to the philosophy of the Declaration.

To understand how far this country has departed from the Declaration of Independence whose bicentennial it so ingenuously celebrates, it will first be necessary to comprehend the roots of relativism in all possible clarity, for which one could hardly do better than to read a few passages from the *Leviathan* of Thomas Hobbes:

> But whatever is the object of any man's appetite or desire, that is it which he for his part calleth *good;* and the object of his hate or aversion, *evil;* and of his contempt, *vile* or *inconsiderable.* For these words of good, evil, and contemptible, are ever used in relation to the person that useth them. . . .[1]

In Hobbes the distinction between man and beast all but disappears. Honor and shame are mere names reducible to pleasure and pain produced by external causes.[2] Reason is reduced to "deliberation," which is merely the "alternate succession of appetites, aversions, hopes and fears, [and] is no less in other living creatures than in man."[3] Anticipating behaviorism, Hobbes rejects the notion of reason or thought as having any initiatory agency constitutive of human aims or purposes. "For the thoughts are to the desires, as scouts, and spies, to range abroad, and find the way to the things desired."[4] From psychological relativism to cultural relativism is but a short step. Again Hobbes:

> *Good* and *evil* are names that signify our appetites, and aversions; which in different tempers, customs, and doctrines of men, are different: and divers men, differ not only in their judgment, on the senses of what is pleasant, and unpleasant to the taste, smell, hearing, touch, and sight; but also of what is conformable, or disagreeable to reason, in the actions of common life.[5]

The essence of this teaching, though less lucidly and pungently expressed, will be found in the writings of Karl Marx. It was a young Marx who wrote in *The German Ideology:*

> [We] do not set out from what men say, imagine, conceive, nor from men as narrated, thought of, imagined, conceived, in order to arrive at men in the flesh. We set out from real, active men, and on the basis of their real life-process we demonstrate the development of the *ideological reflexes* and echoes of this life-process. The *phantoms* formed in the human brain are also, necessarily, *sublimates* of their material life-process, which is empirically verifiable and bound to material premises. Morality, religion, metaphysics, all the rest of ideology and their corresponding forms of consciousness, thus no longer have the semblance of independence.[6] [Italics added]

We are now prepared to explore what is at stake in the conflict between the Declaration of Independence and the present day doctrine of relativism, whatever its form. First, the logical implications.

The Declaration silently yet eloquently affirms the power of reason to apprehend universal moral truths or standards by which to determine whether any form of government is just or unjust. Relativism denies this power of reason. It thereby denies any moral justification for the Revolution or indeed for any revolution. The Declaration derives its standards from the laws of nature. Relativism rejects the notion of natural law or of natural justice. All notions of justice are conventional, fundamentally arbitrary, and the derivatives of sub-rational or of non-rational forces, whether psychological, cultural, or historical. Hence there can be no real moral issues in the conflicts between peoples or nations; there can be neither just wars nor unjust wars. The Declaration proclaims that all men are created equal, meaning that all men are subject to the same universal moral law, as a consequence of which no group of men can rightly rule other men as if they were an inferior species. In contrast, relativism fosters the notion that all values or moralities are in principle equal, from which it follows that free societies are not intrinsically superior to slave societies.

Having considered the logical implications of relativism, I now turn to its psychological consequences.

The Declaration, we saw, presupposes two kinds or functions of reason, one metaphysical, the other pragmatic. Relativism reduces or lowers reason to the pragmatic level. As a result, men become more and more preoccupied with the immediate, with narrow and limited interests. In the process, reason becomes little more than the clever, calculating instrument of the consuming desires. So long as the metaphysical reason had some efficacy, or to the extent that the intuition that man is a metaphysical animal influenced human conduct, a sense of dignity (or of shame) imposed restraints on men's appetites. As men's appetites expand, their intellects shrink. To put the matter another way, with the inevitable decline of honor under the education of moral relativism, there is a corresponding decline in men's respect for reason and truth. Let one generation after another be taught, in opposition to the Declaration, that reason is incapable of discovering universal truths or standards by which to determine whether one form of government is intrinsically superior to another, and the will and determination of that people to persevere in any cause involving death and destruction will be undermined.

Wholehearted dedication to any cause is psychologically impossible among men tainted by moral relativism.

To avoid misunderstanding, I must pause and consider at some length certain peculiarities about the manifestations of relativism in a democratic society. It should first be noted that exceedingly few people have the courage, let alone the intellectual capacity, to be thoroughly consistent moral relativists. That would be nihilism, pure and simple.[7] In fact, most relativists are rather conventional. Thus, while many will openly deny the existence of universal moral truths, hardly anyone would publicly avow the conclusion that "everything is permitted." Few would even go so far as former Justice William O. Douglas who, on one occasion, had the temerity to declare that whether or not one is a masochist or a homosexual is merely a matter of "taste."[8] Consequently, there is no reason to be disconcerted or misled should one find in the writings or utterances of most relativists, especially of those who are elected officials, the semblance of ordinary morality.

A second point to be noted is this. Because relativists contend there are no rational or objective grounds for men's moral or political preferences, it follows that their own moral or political preferences, like everyone else's, are fundamentally arbitrary, mere matters of personal taste. To be sure, in a liberal democracy most relativists will be "liberals." It should be understood, however, that relativism does not logically entail contemporary liberalism. Hence one should not be too surprised to find relativists among "conservatives." Furthermore, a relativist can be, and often is, a "moralist" or secular humanist; and here is where his relativism may become almost invisible even to himself. If he happens to be a moralist—for he could as well be a "realist" or "pragmatist"—the relativist will usually be more vocal than others in his opposition to war. Consistent therewith, he will trivialize and obscure those moral or so-called "ideological" differences between nations which contribute to or exacerbate international conflict.[9] But what kind of morality is really governing this relativist?

Any coherent morality must be rooted in a single principle. The principle may be an ultimate good, a *summum bonum*, toward which one strives, such as happiness; or it may be an ultimate evil, a *summum malum*, from which one flees, such as violent death. Following Hobbes, the relativist cannot possibly accept the former, if only because there is no agreement even among philosophers as to what constitutes happiness. He is therefore compelled, consciously or otherwise, to take his ultimate bearing on the latter, the *summum malum*, if only because the bulk of mankind, under a secular dispensation, will agree with Hobbes that the greatest evil is violent death. And so the relativist who happens to be a moralist will seek peace above all other values.[10] But what is this "peace"? Certainly it is not completeness or fullness of being. Rather, it is little more than the absence of strife, the "little more" being ease and comfort. For it goes without saying that men are not content merely to live; they want to live commodiously. Thus, beneath the surface of the relativistic moralist is a benign hedonism (which is to be expected given the denial that man is a metaphysical animal).

If, however, the relativist happens to be a "realist," he will tend to trivialize and obscure the moral differences between just and unjust regimes by contending that their "ideologies" and appeals to universalist principles are but devices for securing domestic solidarity and international support for what are in fact material interests. What really animates nations is not moral principle but the desire for power. Here the realist is on solid Hobbesian grounds where he joins the moralist.[11] Their difference lies essentially in this: The moralist accepts the empirical or descriptive conclusion of the realist, but only as a contingent and alterable fact of international relations. Here the moralist parts company with Hobbes. He recognizes that the desire for power breeds fear and suspicion among nations and so can lead to the greatest of evils, violent death in war. But he maintains, contrary to Hobbes and most realists, that the desire for power is not an unalterable ingredient of human nature, which is basically benign. (Enter Rousseau.) For the moralist, the desire for power (or aggressiveness generally) is merely a manifestation of human insecurity having its origin either in economic or in psychological deprivation. Universalist moral doctrines, those intolerant, dogmatic ideologies which breed fear and distrust among nations, aggravate this insecurity by stimulating or magnifying the desire for power. Accordingly, the moralist believes more fervently than others that international conflict can at least be minimized by increasing cultural and commercial exchange and cooperation,[12] and by various unilateral demonstrations of good will—all of which are intended to promote greater understanding and prosperity among nations, as well as mutual trust and confidence. The realist, having a less optimistic view of human nature, regards this with some skepticism. Nevertheless, he will admit (though not with complete consistency) that conflicting ideologies do in fact aggravate international tensions. With the moralist, therefore, he would like to *de-ideologize* international relations. In this way his earlier empiricism or descriptivism is imperceptibly transformed into prescriptivism: the "is" becomes the "ought." And so the realist adorns all regimes, including tyrannies, with the mantle of legitimacy. More accurately, he renders the legal just.

By obscuring the distinction between the legal and the just—which is precisely what is involved in attempts to de-ideologize international relations—both realists and moralists seem to be fostering a morality of the status quo. But the truth is more complex, and their efforts are more subtle. For to de-ideologize international relations is to alter, in a fundamental way, what each nation stands for, hence, its very morality. To put the issue in another light:

To render compatible two nations governed by conflicting ideologies, it will be necessary to change their political, social, economic, and, above all, their educational institutions such that the institutions of one nation become more and more similar to those of the other. Only through a process of "convergence" requiring fundamental changes in the way of life of one or the other or both of these nations will it be possible to de-ideologize their relationship. Mutual tolerance would then be the *effect* more than the *cause* of convergence. But whatever the case, calling for mutual tolerance—the panacea of psychologically oriented moralists—obscures the real issue and is in fact a piece of hypocrisy. What the relativistic moralist is really saying is this: *Everyone* should be tolerant like me, should put away his dogmas, his sacred myths! There are no universal truths concerning how men should live. It is senseless—even pathological—to struggle for *nothing*, to die for what does not even exist!

Finally, before concluding this discussion of the various manifestations of relativism in a democratic society, one further point needs emphasis. Whether a relativist is a "liberal" or a "conservative," a "moralist" or a "realist," a "dove" or a "hawk," or some combination thereof—for political preferences are ultimately as fortuitous to him as matters of taste—then, all other things being equal, he cannot possibly be as fully dedicated to a cause as one who believes in the intrinsic justice and universal validity of that cause. As Nietzsche so well understood, relativism, by debasing one's own values, weakens the personality and tends to paralyze the will.[13] Who indeed would undertake great suffering unless he believed in the absolute worth and justice of his cause? In a protracted struggle requiring material sacrifice and the loss of life itself, the relativist's spirit will falter, be he citizen or statesman. Modern men will fight and die for what they believe to be true. But only the deluded would persevere in a struggle for an ideology which cannot be shown to be morally superior to that of any nation which threatens their own. Meanwhile, the democratic statesman tainted by moral relativism will be psychologically undermined (if not crippled) should he have to rally his people against any nation which is a tyranny in fact, but seldom called such by name—especially if the leaders of that tyranny have long propagated, among their own people and the world at large, an ideology which not only professes to embody the truth as to how men should live, but which portrays the democratic nation's way of life as the epitome of evil.

At this point it must be made clear that the preceding discussion, as well as what is to follow, is not intended as a philosophical refutation of relativism. Relativism may or may not be true. But like Nietzsche, I believe I have shown that relativism is deadly.[14] Whatever the case, my purpose, as indicated earlier, is to articulate the principles of the Declaration of Independence in such a way as to facilitate their use as criteria for analyzing and evaluating, from the perspective of the statesmen of 1776, the character of contemporary political thought and practice. This being understood, consider the teachings of J. William Fulbright, former Senator of the United States and Chairman of the Senate Foreign Relations Committee.

II

In his book, *Old Myths and New Realities* (published in 1964), Senator Fulbright refers to the truths of the Declaration as "myths," and he claims that, given the new realities of the atomic age, we cannot afford the "luxury" of those old myths or indeed of any "ideology."[15] Clearly, the Senator's understanding of the relationship between philosophy and action is very different from that which animated the statesmen of the Declaration. In his *Arrogance of Power* (published in 1966), he writes: "I think that man is qualified to contemplate metaphysics but not to practice it."[16] What does he mean by *metaphysics?* All that can be inferred from the context of his statement is that the term is more or less synonymous with *ideology*. What, then, is an *ideology?* An ideology, we later learn, consists of "man's beliefs about how societies should be organized and related to each other."[17] In other words, an ideology is a comprehensive answer to the question of how men should live. From this it follows that while we are qualified to contemplate or inquire into how men should live, we are incapable of putting into practice the findings of our inquiry. Theory must ever remain divorced from practice, philosophy from action.[18] This renders political philosophy a mere academic pursuit irrelevant to politics. Politics becomes a wholly pragmatic affair, the business of the pragmatic reason. As we have seen, however, the pragmatic reason, uninformed by the metaphysical reason, tends to become preoccupied with immediate wants and transient interests. The result is a trivialization of politics (and of political science). Here, a word from John Stuart Mill is instructive:

> A person must have a very unusual taste for intellectual exercise in and for itself, who will put himself to the trouble of thought when it is to have no outward effect, or qualify himself for functions which he has no chance of being allowed to exercise. The only sufficient incitement to mental exertion, in any but a few minds in a generation, is the prospect of some practical use to be made of its results.[19]

Not that a nation governed by men who sever theory from practice will be wholly destitute of intellectual power. Rather, it will be ruled increasingly by narrow technicians and mediocrities. To divorce philosophy from politics cannot but lead to a narrowing of men's intellectual and moral horizons, thereby lowering the standards of political life.

But the truth is that Senator Fulbright does not really

believe we are qualified to contemplate metaphysics, that is, to apprehend universal truths concerning how men should live or how societies should be organized. He tells us that "the sources of ideological belief are largely accidental and irrational."[20] This being the case, there are no rational standards by which to determine whether one nation's way of life is preferable to another's; the belief that the principles and purposes of government enunciated in the Declaration of Independence are intrinsically superior to those which govern the Soviet Union has no rational basis. Further, in the opinion of Mr. Fulbright, the conviction that such "myths" or "ideologies" are true—or that the principles and purposes of one's own nation are morally superior to those of another—is precisely what engenders international tension and war. If, therefore, the sources of ideological belief are largely accidental and irrational, then, in the words of the Senator, "the causes . . . of war have more to do with pathology than with politics, more to do with irrational pride and pain [feelings of national inferiority?], than with rational calculations of advantage and profit."[21] Hence it would seem that just as we are incapable of truly knowing what ends or causes men ought to live for, so are we incapable of knowing what ends or causes may be worth dying for—unless the pedestrian phrase, "rational calculations of advantage and profit," is indicative of some metaphysical principle.

Be this as it may, it is tempting to say that calculations of advantage and profit describe Senator Fulbright's prescriptions for American foreign policy. How curious. For such calculations are also descriptive of contemporary capitalism. Generally speaking, today's capitalist does not allow political abstractions or ideologies to obstruct his commercial relations with other nations. Committed to laissez-faire, he accepts the world as it is, with all its different forms of government. He is tolerant, he is accommodating. And tolerance and accommodation reward him with material advantage and profit. This happens to be the very language of Senator Fulbright's foreign policy. It is, he contends and emphasizes, "a *conservative* policy" (italics in the original) intended to save the world from nuclear catastrophe. Such a policy calls for "tolerance" and "accommodation," more precisely, for "an approach that accepts the world as it is, with all its existing nations and ideologies."[22] This, of course, describes the policy of "détente" whose most ardent (or at least most obvious) supporters, however, are "liberals." We thus behold the paradox of liberals trying to save the world from nuclear disaster by applying the morality (or the moral indifference) of laissez-faire capitalism to present-day international relations! Not that I here question the wisdom of such a policy,* but I do wish to reveal its genealogy, or should I say its underlying psychology? That policy is animated by the fear of violent death; it is based on what Senator Fulbright calls a "politics of survival."† If we pursue such a politics now, says the Senator, we may in time find that we can do better than just survive. We may find that the simple preference for life and peace has an inspirational force of its own, less intoxicating perhaps than the sacred abstraction of nation and ideology, but far more relevant to

*Although Antony C. Sutton does not draw this conclusion, the moral relativism of contemporary capitalism helps to explain his *Western Technology and Soviet Economic Development 1917–1930* (Stanford: Hoover Institution Publications, 1968), which argues convincingly that "Soviet economic development for 1917–1930 was essentially dependent on Western technological aid" (p. 283), and that *"At least 95 percent of the industrial structure* received this aid" (p. 348, italics in the original).

†The Senator's "politics of survival" tends to confirm his own contention that the sources of ideological doctrines are largely irrational. The *sources* may or may not be irrational. What really counts, however, is whether any particular doctrine is defensible when examined rationally. Professor Henry A. Kissinger once thought that a "politics of survival" is ultimately "destructive of purpose and values." See his *The Necessity for Choice* (New York: Harper & Row, 1961), p. 289, and below, p. 40 n.

the requirements of human life and happiness."[23] Not mere survival, but life plus ease and comfort appear to be the highest aims of Senator Fulbright's foreign policy. This recalls the worldly wisdom of Hobbes: "The passions that incline men to peace are the fear of [violent] death [and the] desire of such things as are necessary to commodious living."[24] But as everybody knows, some people are more fearful of death than others. Accordingly, *only let American statesmen convey, in one manner or another, that violent death is the greatest evil, and this nation will be subject (if it has not already been) to nuclear blackmail*—indeed, to the eventual tyranny of a nation whose leaders have shown utter contempt for human life, including the lives of their own people.*

It is not my purpose to denigrate Senator Fulbright but rather to show how his thoughts on foreign policy have been influenced by relativism. Thus, consider the American and Vietnamese revolutions, the one against the English, the other against the French. A relativist would tend to obscure the moral differences between these two revolutions, hence the principles or purposes guiding Washington and those guiding Ho Chi Minh. Perhaps he would refer to both revolutions as struggles for independence against colonial rule, or even as "wars of national liberation." He would ignore or obscure the fact that one revolution sought a new form of liberty, the other a new form of servitude. Such obfuscation frequently occurs in the hearings of the

---

*See *The Necessity for Choice*, p. 86, where Professor Kissinger once understood that "against an opponent known to consider nuclear war as the worst evil, nuclear blackmail is an almost foolproof strategy." Also in the once considered opinion of Professor Kissinger, "Whenever peace—conceived as the avoidance of war—has been the primary objective of a power or a group of powers, the international system has been at the mercy of the most ruthless member of the international community." See his *A World Restored: Metternich, Castlereagh, and the Problems of Peace 1812-1822* (Boston: Houghton Mifflin Co., 1973), pp. 1-3.

Senate Foreign Relations Committee. For example, in the 1966 hearings on Vietnam, Senator Fulbright, trying to teach the public that the American Revolution was not fundamentally different from its Vietnamese counterpart, posed the following rhetorical question to General Maxwell Taylor: "How do you describe the war of 1776? Was that a war of national liberation, or wasn't it?"[25] The same implicit relativism may be seen in the following remarks of Senator Fulbright questioning the wisdom of continued economic assistance to South Korea in 1970:

> What is it that is so important [in that area of the world]? What difference does it make finally when you get down to it, whether South Korea rules North [Korea] or North rules South?[26]

Presumably, any consideration of the ideological differences between North and South Korea would interfere with those "rational calculations of advantage and profit" referred to earlier. Indeed, ideological considerations would be pathological, rooted in irrational pride or "intolerant puritanism" or "self-righteousness." This puritanism, Senator Fulbright contends, has been aroused in the United States by Communism, that is, by our belief that "communism is a barbarous philosophy utterly devoid of redeeming features of humanity."[27] Senator Fulbright makes no effort to refute this belief. Instead he calls for a foreign policy based on "democratic humanism." Democratic humanism is supposedly compatible with accepting the world as it is. Accordingly, a foreign policy based on democratic humanism requires moral indifference as to whether North Korea rules South Korea, or vice versa. Such indifference is necessary to save the world from nuclear war.

The foreign policy described above combines, in a curious way, the "realist" (or "pragmatist") and "moralist" manifestations of the doctrine of moral relativism. It should be evident, however, that such realism is not very realistic, and such moralism is not very moral. Nothing could more

effectively erode the moral fabric of this nation and therefore the nation's survival than to apply the moral relativism
implicit in contemporary capitalism to the conduct of
American foreign policy. Yet Senator Fulbright rhetorically
asks his readers: "Are we to regard communist countries
as more or less normal states with whom we can have more
or less normal relations, or are we to regard them indiscriminately as purveyors of an evil ideology with whom we
can never reconcile [sic]?"[28] To this Alexander Solzhenitsyn
might reply:

> In keeping silent about evil, in burying it so deep within us that no
> sign of it appears on the surface, we are implanting it, and it will
> rise up a thousandfold in the future. When we neither punish nor
> reproach evildoers, we are not simply protecting their trivial old
> age, we are thereby ripping the foundations of justice from beneath
> new generations. It is for this reason, and not because of the
> "weakness of indoctrinational work," that they are growing up
> "indifferent." Young people are acquiring the conviction that foul
> deeds are never punished on earth, that they always bring pros-
> perity.
>
> It is going to be uncomfortable, horrible, to live in such a
> country![29]

This passage, from *The Gulag Archipelago*, refers to the fact
that not one of those responsible for the tortures and deaths
of countless millions in Soviet slave labor camps has ever
been brought to trial or even publicly reproached by the
successors of Stalin. Those monstrous labor camps, first
constructed by Lenin, are still being used under the Brezhnev regime. But more to the point, Solzhenitsyn attributes
the extermination of some sixty-six million Russians not
simply to Marxist ideology, but to moral relativism, com-
paring Russia under Marxism to an earlier age "when
morality was not considered relative and when the distinction between good and evil was very simply perceived by
the heart."[30]

But there is yet another and, for the non-communist world, a more ominous consequence of remaining silent about evil. Statesmen who say nothing about the true character, methods, and strategic objectives of the Soviet Union lead the public to believe that the Kremlin harbors no hostile designs upon the free world.* Perhaps more than any other single factor this silence, a product of relativism, led to the defeat of the United States in the Vietnam War and to the resignation of Lyndon Johnson from the Presidency in 1968 upon his failure to sustain public support for his Administration's policy in Southeast Asia. An ironic end, for in reflecting on his conduct of the Presidency, Mr. Johnson wrote in his memoirs:

> The first step I took as President in my effort to improve East-West relations was to insist that we avoid wherever possible the harsh name-calling of the Cold War era. Those exchanges of ideological rhetoric accomplished nothing except to stir up angry emotions on both sides. Throughout my administration we . . . refrained from using such phrases as "captive nations" and "ruthless totalitarians."[32]

The naiveté of this statement—as if an imperialistic regime

---

*The Soviet Union employs what may be termed an "octagonal" strategy of protracted war. This strategy orchestrates military and economic, ideological and semantic, cultural and psychological, and political and diplomatic factors so as to produce on a targeted country increasing pressure which, reaching unbearable levels, eventually brings about its disintegration and collapse. The method, in the words of a recent Soviet handbook, "is the uninterrupted attack; its means, prolonged operational pursuit, which avoids pauses and stops, and is attained by a succession of consecutive operations, each of which serves as a transitional link toward the ultimate goal [which is] the complete annihilation of the vital forces of the enemy." "Détente" or "peaceful coexistence" is but a "transitional link" intended to hasten that goal. It is a disarming tactic enabling the Soviet Union to procure Western trade and technology. It is aimed at buying time, with Western compliance, for the Russians to gain strategic nuclear superiority, which they have in fact achieved.[31]

based on the primacy of force could be moderated by covering up its evil designs—is remarkable. But the point is this: by failing to enlighten the American people about the geostrategic objectives of the Soviet Union (for example, by not revealing how Moscow was arming and using its client, North Vietnam, to disengage the United States from Southeast Asia), American statesmen have abandoned one of the cardinal principles of the Declaration. I mean the principle that requires statesmen to educate public opinion. I am speaking of a republic. To conduct the foreign policy of a republic effectively requires solid and sustained public support. Such support will not be forthcoming unless the people understand that they cannot long enjoy the blessings of liberty in an international environment hostile to the republican form of government. A President must therefore show them, graphically and in geopolitical terms, how Communist Russia, a regime of unmitigated evil, is penetrating Southeast Asia, the Indian Ocean, the Middle East, Africa, and Latin America in its relentless drive toward global ascendency.

In remaining silent about evil, American statesmen have been engaged in an impossible as well as self-destructive undertaking: they have attempted to de-ideologize—I am tempted to say de-moralize—international relations in general, and American foreign policy in particular.* This refusal to acknowledge and confront evil candidly and courageously may be traced to the fear of violent death and to the pervasive and subtle influence of moral relativism.

Finally, let us look at what may prove to be the most fateful manifestation of moral relativism. This passage is

---

*In his press conference of July 16, 1975, Secretary Kissinger suggested it would be unwise for President Ford to meet with the exiled Solzhenitsyn, because such a meeting with the outspoken critic of the Soviet Union and of American foreign policy would jeopardize "détente." On those feeble grounds, anyone who is *persona non grata* at the Kremlin would become *persona non grata* at the White House—a pretty commentary on the bicentennial of America's independence.

from the *Basic Principles of Relations Between the United States of America and the Union of Soviet Socialist Republics*, signed by Richard M. Nixon and Leonid Brezhnev at the Moscow Conference of May, 1972, concluding the SALT I Agreements:

> Differences in ideology and in the social systems of the U.S.A. and the U.S.S.R. are not obstacles to the bilateral development of normal relations based on the principles of sovereignty, non-interference in internal affairs and mutual advantage.[33]

This statement reappeared, somewhat revised, in Mr. Nixon's report to a joint session of Congress delivered upon his return from the Moscow Conference:

> Recognizing that the quest for useful knowledge transcends the differences between ideologies and social systems, we have agreed to expand United States and Soviet co-operation in many areas of science and technology.

Diverse indeed are the unwitting disciples of Hobbes. For what, in effect, was Mr. Nixon telling the American people but this: Because comfortable self-preservation transcends differences between ideologies and social systems, we have agreed to expand United States and Soviet co-operation in many areas of science and technology. Still, if it is true that the quest for useful knowledge does transcend such differences, then one could as well substitute Nazi Germany for the Soviet Union. In fact, given the respective quality of science and technology under those two tyrannies, the substitution of Nazi Germany would be more consistent with "rational calculations of advantage and profit." What must be accentuated, however, is this. Mr. Nixon's statement subordinates morality to material interests and thereby trivializes the social and ideological differences between the United States and the Soviet Union; the one a liberal democracy, the other a tyranny whose rulers, in the words of Bernard Lewis, "recognize no motive but interest and fear, no methods but guile and force."[34] Whether, or to what extent, Mr. Nixon is a conscious relativist may be left open. Nevertheless, his mode of thought may be designated as "crypto-relativism" to distinguish it from purer varieties.

To avoid oversimplifying the matter, I should point out that the question of whether the United States ought to expand cooperation with the Soviet Union in science and technology cannot rightly be decided simply by reference to some moral principle, no more than could the statesmen of the Declaration decide by moral principle alone whether to sever political relations with Great Britain.* These are indeed moral matters; but they should be decided not by moral *principles* so much as by moral *judgment*. We must avoid dogmatism, as did the statesmen of the Declaration of Independence. This leads me to anticipate certain objections which will be raised against the preceding argument.

III

I have said, in effect, that contemporary political thought and practice is inclined more toward relativism than toward the universalism of the Declaration of Independence. I have also said that relativism is deadly, that it undermines wholehearted dedication to any cause. No doubt the relativist will contend that whereas relativism breeds tolerance, universalism breeds intolerance, hence war. But the truth is that relativism provides no rational grounds for preferring tolerance to intolerance, or for that matter, peace to war. What the relativist calls "tolerance" is often a facade for moral indifference. Nor is this all. By denying the power of

*But see above, p. 39 n. From Sutton's persuasive study one could reasonably conclude that, were it not for the transfer of Western technology to the Soviet Union, the regime might have collapsed from the weight of its own tyranny. The consequences of such a collapse for subsequent history staggers the mind. It may not be out of place, therefore, to recall Lenin's saying that the bourgeois would provide the rope with which to hang themselves.

human reason to apprehend universal moral truths, relativism entails a moral pluralism which "justifies" the imposition of one nation's morality upon another—in fact tyranny. Stated another way, whereas the universalism of the Declaration embraces mankind as a single species subject to one moral law, relativism fragments humanity into a multiplicity of different species each possessing its own morality, each, therefore, subject to no higher law than its own will. Consequently, one species may feel perfectly justified in dominating another. Far from breeding tolerance, those who propagate the doctrine that all moralities are equally valid are unwittingly fostering among individuals, groups, and nations alike a petty, self-enclosed and self-justifying egoism, thereby contributing to unrelieved intolerance. In contrast, the universalism of the Declaration, because it is based on philosophic reason on the one hand, and civility on the other, is fully aware that not all peoples possess the intellectual, moral, and material endowments required for rendering them fit to receive, to their immediate betterment, the kind of government envisioned by the Declaration. Opposed to doctrinairism (and imperialism), the universalism of the Declaration reflects the thought of urbane, philosophically tempered statesmen too self-confident to impose their wisdom on others. It is the lack of self-confidence that generates moral fanaticism at one extreme, and moral relativism or indifferentism at the other. Both are symptoms of weakness. All the more reason, therefore, to recall the wise words of Whitehead: "On the whole, tolerance is more often found in connection with a genial orthodoxy."[35] Let us now pursue a more philosophical analysis of the issue.

The universal validity ascribed to the Declaration's principles does not entail the doctrinaire imposition of those principles on nations whose traditions and circumstances differ from those of the United States. There are at least three reasons why.*

First, whether we look to the Declaration or to the Constitution, we see that the prescribed ends of government are single terms whose meaning is not univocal. To be sure, such ends as liberty and justice bear a fund of connotations which more or less inform public and private conduct. Nevertheless, ambiguity remains, if only because language is elliptical. Ambiguity makes it possible for diverse men to agree to a common course of action for different reasons.[36] Stated another way: the fact that the meaning of liberty and justice is not *explicit* (or made an object of controversy) makes it possible for diverse men to resolve their differences by discussing the *means* by which those ends may be realized. But inasmuch as those means may be *institutions*, vagueness of ends (qualified by common sense meanings) allows for a considerable variety of more or less compatible forms of government.

The second reason may be traced to the definition of man as *homo rationalis et civilis*. Consider the power of reason. It is, above all, a synthesizing power which seeks to comprehend the connectedness of all things. The claim of reason is that "all things great and small are conceivable as exemplifications of general principles which reign throughout the natural order."[37] The criterion of rationality thus involves comprehensiveness. Applied to politics, this means that reason requires each nation to incorporate the accumulated wisdom of its past into the on-going life of the present. And yet reason is also a *creative* power, such

*A fourth reason is implicitly discussed in Chapter 4, where the relationship between moral principles and moral judgment or prudence is considered. Here, it suffices to point out that while the statesmen of the Declaration proclaim certain absolute rights, they also suggest that the full enjoyment of these rights ought not, under all circumstances, to be insisted upon: "Prudence, indeed, will dictate that Governments long established should not be changed for light and transient causes. . . ."

that the process of incorporation inevitably involves selection, which is to say emphasis and de-emphasis. To put the matter differently: the past consists of a welter of data—of diverse values and relationships—pressing on the present, but not wholly determinative of the issue. There are divergent possibilities or alternatives; there is room for choice, for decision. Reason is that creative agency which makes actual what hitherto was only possible or potential. It introduces novelty into the world by selective emphasis. But reason is also corrective of its own initial selectivity. The self-correction of reason is the soul's civility, its capacity to entertain diverse points of view in its quest for comprehensiveness or fullness of being. Thus, insofar as each nation orders its life primarily on rational instead of customary foundations (following the example of the United States), it would still retain its distinctive character, for it would incorporate its past into a more comprehensive whole for the future. Again, this would allow for a considerable variety of regimes whose institutions need not— and ought not—imitate our own.

The third reason resides in the meaning of what constitutes a universal as opposed to a particular. Following Whitehead, I reject the traditional antithesis common to both classical and modern thought. Here is Whitehead's position as formulated in *Process and Reality:*

> The [traditional] notion of a universal is of that which can enter into the description of many particulars; whereas the notion of a particular is that it is described by universals, and does not itself enter into the description of any other particular. [To the contrary:] An actual entity cannot be described, even inadequately, by universals; because other actual entities do enter into the description of any one actual entity [with greater or lesser degree of relevance]. Thus every so-called 'universal' is particular in the sense of being just what it is, diverse from everything else; and every so-called 'particular' is universal in the sense of entering into the constitutions of other actual entities.[38]

The consequence of this teaching is that, even if it should so desire, no nation can live by principles identical to those of any other nation precisely because of the immanence of its past in the present, a past which enters into the meaning and efficacy of any institutional forms which one nation may borrow from another. To be sure, force or coercion may be employed in attempting to transform a people's way of life according to some universalistic model (as when the Bolsheviks sought to transform Tzarist Russia into a Communist regime). But force can only modify or attenuate, it cannot eliminate, the immanence of the past in the present. (Besides, mere force is repellent to the principle of *homo rationalis et civilis* on which the American republic is based.) Finally, the principle of federalism, intrinsic to the American republic, is incompatible with doctrinairism. The mere notion of *e pluribus unum*—of the many entering into the character of the one and the one entering into the character of the many—exemplifies the non-doctrinaire character of American universalism. This non-univocal universalism is a genial orthodoxy tolerant of a considerable variety of regimes, so long as they are not based on force.

But let us linger a while on the theme of a genial orthodoxy, which calls to mind the wisdom of Pascal who said that we know too little to be dogmatists and too much to be skeptics.

A genial orthodoxy recognizes that the universe is infinitely more subtle and comprehensive than the deliverances of our intellects. From this we learn modesty and magnanimity. On the other hand, a genial orthodoxy presupposes (as does science itself) that the universe is an intelligible whole, that "the ultimate natures of things lie together in a harmony which excludes mere arbitrariness."[39] Thus understood, a genial orthodoxy instills a quiet but manly confidence in the power of reason to apprehend truths transcending the vicissitudes and diversities of time and place, truths of abiding and of universal significance. The statesmen of the Declaration of Independence referred to such truths as "Laws of Nature and of Nature's God." These laws are but recurring patterns of behaviors distinguishing things, yet relating them to one another. Some of these laws or recurring patterns distinguish human behavior from sub-human behavior, for which reason their apprehension is indispensable for a critical as well as constructive approach to the question of how men should live or of how societies should be governed. It is evident, however, that the recurring things never recur in exact detail. Accordingly, what are called laws of nature (and, therefore, the question of how men should live) do not seem to admit of final and univocal articulation. Novelty upsets the definitive conclusions of reason. Yet novelty entails contrast, and contrast involves the unavoidable notion of better and worse. But the notion of better and worse presupposes some standard, a standard of what is best—again, an ideal or perfection to be aimed at, but which mankind, fallible as well as mortal, can never fully realize. These thoughts find exemplification in the seemingly paralogistic phraseology of the Preamble of the American Constitution, namely, "to form a more perfect Union."

There may be no final and univocal articulation of how societies should be governed, but it does not follow that all articulations are equally arbitrary, or that the political principles of one society are no more valid than those of another. Unfortunately, relativism emphasizes the diversities existing among mankind, while retreating various uniformities which distinguish the human from the sub-human into an omitted background. Notice, however, that even sheer diversity, which admittedly is as unavoidable as the *principium individuationis*, lends ontological support for a liberal society. In addition, epistemological support for a liberal society may be derived from the inescapable selective emphasis and self-corrective power of the finite intellect, which confirms the principle of individuality on the one hand, and suggests the freedom of the intellect on the other. Furthermore, the standard for judging the merits of one society over another is implicit in the very notion of selectivity, namely, *comprehensiveness*. By this I mean that that society is best which brings into mutual coordination and intensification the greatest range of human values, such that freedom dwells with virtue, equality with excellence, wealth with beauty, the here and now with the eternal. Suitably articulated, this range of values would constitute a genial orthodoxy compatible with the Declaration of Independence.

Four   On Force and Revolution

I am certainly not an advocate for frequent and untried changes in
laws and constitutions. I think moderate imperfections had better
be borne with, because, when once known, we accommodate
ourselves to them and find practical means of correcting their ill
effects. But I know also that laws and institutions must go hand in
hand with the progress of the human mind. | Thomas Jefferson
That the people have an original right to establish, for their future
government, such principles as, in their opinion, shall most conduce
to their own happiness, is the basis on which the whole American
fabric has been created. The exercise of this original right is a
very great exertion; nor can it, nor ought it, to be frequently
repeated. | Chief Justice John Marshall

I HAVE suggested that genuine tolerance is inseparable
from civility. Civility requires us to pay "a decent
respect to the opinions of mankind," to opinions
which differ from our own. But to respect the opinions of
others, or to have the incentive to study them seriously,
we must assume that their opinions may be true or partly
true, hence, that we may have to discard or modify our own
opinions, and perhaps even alter our way of life. But
suppose we conclude after reflection that certain opinions
of others are more or less erroneous. As decent men we may
feel obliged to state our reasons for thinking so, especially
if we and they are fellow citizens whose different opinions
happen to concern the justice of certain acts of our own
government. But there could hardly be any point in
engaging in such controversy if the parties involved, having
been taught by moral relativists, believed that all opinions
concerning justice are subjective, that there are no rational
or objective standards by which to determine whether the
opinions of one group are morally preferable to those of

another. Indeed, it would be misleading to speak of those opinions as opinions: they would merely be likes and dislikes, as arbitrary as the preferences of our palates.[1] The relativist resolves such differences in one of three ways, though at times distinctions between any two are cloudy.

The first is this. So long as no one group possesses a monopoly of power, disputes will be resolved by bargaining (which is not to be confused with compromise).[2] Of course, there will be a tendency in each group to make extreme demands. With the eclipse of the metaphysical intellect, reason becomes merely the instrument of men's appetites; and with the corresponding decline of honor, men become less motivated by the "common good" or the "public interest" (notions equivalent to "justice" but which relativists regard as fictions).

The second method of resolving group conflict may loosely be termed "blackmail" or "extortion." It occurs when one group refuses to perform some vital function unless its demands are satisfied. In a highly complex and interdependent society "blackmail" is especially effective because it can bring the entire system to a standstill.

The third method of resolving conflict is the use of brute force. In a relativistic society, any group believing it can succeed need have no scruples in attempting to seize political power and suppress its opponents. And here we see that the tolerance fostered by relativism is a facade for impotence and petty egoism. There are those who encourage tolerance in order to be tolerated. Beneath the skin of the tolerant relativist may lurk the intolerant tyrant whose ascendency only awaits a different correlation of forces.[3]

Notice that in the three methods of resolving conflict, bargaining, "blackmail," and brute force, there is a progressive decline of reason. These three methods reflect three successive stages by which moral and intellectual anarchy culminate in undisguised tyranny. By the time of the second stage, Hamilton's question "whether societies of men are really capable or not of establishing good government from reflection and choice" must be answered in the negative: "they are forever destined to depend for their political constitution on accident and force."

And yet, was not this nation conceived in a violent revolution, a revolution whose meaning is articulated by a Declaration rooted in what I have called the metaphysical reason? Admitting, therefore, that relativism does not minimize (let alone preclude) the use of force, may not the same be said of any universalism such as that embodied in the Declaration? Before this question can be answered, some preliminary considerations are necessary.

First note that relativism, when logically consistent, is ethically neutral concerning the use of force. The trouble is that force, or some form of coercion, is an unavoidable aspect of political life. For that reason alone politics is not and cannot be ethically neutral. Why is coercion ineluctable? One reason is because men are not angels. As Madison has written: "If men were angels, no government would be necessary."[4] But there is another reason, well understood by Madison, why government is necessary. It stems from the obvious fact that men are not born equal in their intellectual, moral, and physical endowments. Given what Madison called the "diversity of the faculties of men" (among which he included "perception, judgment, desire, volition, memory, [and] imagination"),[5] and given the additional fact that nature does not enable mankind to live and enjoy life without labor, then, to state the problem negatively, some men—the avaricious and the ambitious as well as the envious and the indolent—will seek to take advantage of their fellows. For this reason, if for no other, government is needed to prevent the few from oppressing the many, and to prevent the many from oppressing the few. This will necessitate some form of coercion. The only question is what kind of government is best designed to reduce the role of unjust coercion in human affairs. (Such a government would also enlarge the role of reason or persuasion in human affairs.) Since coercion can originate in society at large—recall that stage of society where conflicts were resolved by the method of "blackmail"—too weak a government can endanger liberty as surely as one that is too strong.

It should be evident that moral relativism cannot answer these crucial questions on rational grounds. Will a government influenced by the teaching of moral relativism be more or less coercive than a government influenced by the teachings of the Declaration of Independence? It may be either. It depends wholly on chance, on the accidents of personality, or on some fortuitous constellation of forces. If, therefore, American government has not been too coercive, gratitude may be owed not to twentieth-century relativism, but rather to that eighteenth-century universalism embodied in the Declaration, which continues to cultivate, albeit with progressively diminishing force, that respect for reason which inspires greatness, and that civility which renders greatness humane.

Still, it needs to be emphasized, however obvious it may be, that the universalism of the Declaration does not prohibit the use of force. Again, "whenever any Form of Government becomes destructive of [their unalienable rights] it is the Right of the People to alter or to *abolish* it" (italics added). But it must also be emphasized that the Declaration, consistent with the civility and philosophic temperament of its authors, sanctions the use of force only as a last resort. There are good reasons for this. One is that revolutions encourage not only the nobler, but also the baser passions of men, and may as readily end in tyranny as in liberty. This is why "Governments long established should not be changed for light and transient causes." Before resorting to force for correcting abuses of government, civilized men will appeal to reason and even to sentiment. Thus, in the

Declaration's "denunciation," the statesmen of the Revolution recall that

> In every stage of these oppressions We have Petitioned for Redress in the most humble terms. . . . Nor have We been wanting in attentions to our British brethren. . . . We have appealed to their native justice and magnanimity, and we have conjured them by the ties of our common kindred to disavow these usurpations. . . . They, too, have been deaf to the voice of justice and consanguinity. We must, therefore, acquiesce in the necessity, which denounces our Separation, and hold them, as we hold the rest of mankind, Enemies in War, in Peace Friends.

As men of honor who preferred liberty to servility, the statesmen of the Declaration had no alternative but to remedy their grievances by arms.

Not simply honor, however, but reason itself requires the use of force when no other remedy is availing. At such times, in other words, the use of force is a rational as well as moral imperative. In a world where not all nations are governed by the civility of the Declaration, those which are so governed are obliged to employ might in order to uphold right. To pursue, instead, a policy of pacifism would only insure the victory of the wicked. The countries which have most need of pacifists incarcerate them; pacifists thrive only in countries which have least need of their benighted persuasion.* In our time, there is a powerful tendency among certain people to believe that right cannot remain right when invested with force, that the use of force on behalf of justice makes one morally suspect. A directly related tendency is to believe that the just person or nation must be the weaker, the victim. People of this persuasion usually assume that justice is benevolence, and that benevolence alone is sufficient to disarm evil. There is, of course, the opposite error of believing that evil can be

---

*The most succinct reply to pacifism is Kipling's "making mock of uniforms that guard you while you sleep."[6]

eliminated merely by the application of brute power. Actually, both schools share the same misconception about the nature of power.

Metaphysically, every entity manifests power, since it is more or less constitutive of every other entity. And nothing is more powerful than *thought* since, more than any other entity, thought transcends space and time. A nation may have great military power and be lacking in great intellectual and moral power, and vice versa. Yet this can be misleading. For the possession of great military power— think of the Soviet Union—is alone indicative of certain intellectual and moral virtues, such as scientific knowledge and foresight, discipline and courage. All other things being equal, therefore, power has a claim to rule or to dispense justice. Not that might makes right. It would be truer to say that right makes might. But the truth is more complex. Justice without power is less than justice; power without justice is less than powerful.

To say that the use of force is, under certain circumstances, a rational as well as moral imperative is to admit a *natural* right to revolution. The right to revolution is but an extension of the right of self-defense or self-preservation. There is no need, however, to follow Hobbes and limit the meaning of self-preservation to mere physical survival. We do not regard ourselves as mere bodies, as is obvious from our notion of self-respect or honor. Nor, as with Hobbes and moderns generally, should the self be regarded atomistically.[7] The self is a center of purposes. The pursuit of these purposes may be regarded as so many streams of energy radiating from the center of the self and differentially modulating the opinions, passions, and interests of all other individuals composing the community. The self is therefore a center of diverse relationships and values the coordination of which depends largely on various political institutions and formal skills developed over the course of time. Consequently, self-preservation requires the preservation of the entire self, including the political whole of which it is a part. It follows that the right of self-preservation extends from the individual to the nation as a whole.

The same conclusion may be arrived at more simply and directly. Thus, because we are created beings who have not created ourselves, beings, moreover, who have been created equal, we are equally obliged to secure the rights with which we have been equally endowed. To secure these rights (the Declaration also calls them *ends*) various forms of government are established among men; and as noted earlier, the forms are means designed to achieve these ends. Now it was at this point that the Declaration drew the conclusion "That whenever any Form of Government becomes destructive of those ends, it is the Right of the People"—also referred to as their *duty*—"to alter or abolish it." Obviously the fulfillment of that duty may require revolution.

This conclusion is but a consequence of the natural law which, as already suggested, is both rational and moral. Because men are entitled to pursue certain ends, they are entitled to employ means *proportioned* to those ends.[8] The ends, I am afraid to say, *do* justify the means: nothing but ends *can* justify means. Those who claim that the ends do not justify the means—and specifically that force must always be avoided—do so in the name of an end, such as "peace" or the "right of self-determination." To say, however, that nothing but ends can justify means is not to say that the end justifies *any* means. The key term is "proportion." The only way in which the means can be proportioned to the ends is if the ends inform the means, otherwise the means would be meaningless or irrational. The importance of this truth under a relativistic dispensation can hardly be exaggerated. The issue is the use of force as a means of achieving certain ends. For the ends to inform the means, the ends must be comprehensively understood. A single means, such as military force, may be employed for opposite ends. One people may use such force to achieve liberty, another to stifle liberty. "It is not the inherent nature of actions," says Aristotle, "but the end or object for which they are done, which makes one action differ from another in the way of honour and dishonour."[9] It is one thing to use force on behalf of a noble cause, another on behalf of an ignoble cause. It follows that the courage of soldiers who fight for a just country is qualitatively different from the courage of soldiers who fight, however sincerely, for an unjust country.

This will no doubt be received with distaste by certain humanitarians who wish to make sincerity an unqualified virtue, or who would like us to believe that "idealism" abstracted from the character of the ideal is self-justifying. However, precisely because man is a metaphysical animal, all of man's so-called *moral* virtues, including courage, must be assimilated to the metaphysical reason. Otherwise there would be no essential difference between the courage of a man defending his children and the courage of a lion defending its cubs. To the contrary, except in abstraction from the whole, not a single human function can rightly be identified with its animal counterpart, as the notion of privacy and the sense of shame should indicate.

The metaphysical principle operating here has been anticipated: Just as the part is constitutive of the whole, so the whole is constitutive of the part. (For example: A molecule of oxygen in the atmosphere is not identical to a molecule of oxygen in our lungs. Similarly, the physical desires of a human being differ from the physical desires of an animal.) To be consistent, therefore, the original statement regarding means and ends will have to be modified: the ends do indeed inform the means, but the means are in turn determinative of the ends. Stated another way, the means are the ends in process of realization. What is ordinarily termed means and ends are static abstractions; useful, but politically and philosophically misleading.

This being so, it was misleading to say that the same means, such as force, can be used for morally opposed ends. When a thief mortally wounds a policeman who in turn mortally wounds the thief, two deaths have occurred, both by force. Yet the policeman was upholding the law which supports the moral principle that it is wrong to take from others what is rightfully their own. The thief violated that principle of natural law or justice.[10] Should we not then distinguish his act from that of the policeman in terms of their conflicting ends? The policeman employed *force*, the thief *violence*. When force is used for unjust ends it ceases to be force and becomes violence. Furthermore, anyone who takes from others what is rightfully their own violates the fundamental principle of natural law that all men are created equal: it is as if he were treating others as an inferior species, thereby severing the moral bands which have connected him with mankind. For by treating others as if they were animals, he has made himself like an animal; that is, by his violence upon others he has given others just cause for using force upon him.

At this point it should be noted that the error of saying that the same means can be used for fundamentally opposed ends exemplifies what Whitehead calls the "fallacy of misplaced concreteness."[11] The intellect necessarily abstracts. Here it abstracts from a whole which includes ends and which endows means, such as force, with meaning. Also, ends are means to higher ends. Note the order of ends referred to in the Declaration: life, liberty, and happiness. Life is an end, but not an end in itself, and the same may be said of liberty. What is an end in itself is happiness, whose content is not arbitrary or merely a matter of personal taste.* John Adams

---

*Consider once more the Declaration's proclaiming the people's right to "institute new Government . . . as to them shall seem most likely to effect their Safety and Happiness." Contrary to many conservatives and "Straussians," the statesmen of the Declaration seem to have held that it is the purpose of government to bring about or produce happiness or to assist in its realization. This is a positive view of government which recalls the teachings of classical political philosophy. It greatly enlarges the sphere of statesmanship and makes possible an architectonic politics.

wrote: "All sober inquiries after truth, ancient and modern, pagan and Christian, have declared the happiness of man, as well as his dignity, consists in virtue."[12] To be borne in mind is that the Declaration, as we have seen, presupposes a hierarchical universe in which man stands between beast and God. The manner in which man pursues happiness, *which itself will reveal the meaning or content of happiness*, must be consistent with his own nature, with those qualities which distinguish the human from the sub-human: the metaphysical reason and the virtue of civility. It follows that should men be compelled to use force to secure happiness, the force must be modulated by the promptings of the metaphysical reason in cooperation with the restraining power of civility.

Of course, human reason is not infallible. With the best of intentions men sometimes use force when its use is unnecessary; and, conversely, even without the influence of cowardice and sentimentality, men sometimes fail to use force when its use is necessary. As for the degree or kind of force which may be required on a given occasion, again it must be proportioned to the end in view (with the end understood, so far as possible, in relation to long-range as well as immediate consequences). Should controversy arise over the use or degree of force required to achieve a particular end, say liberty, then, ordinary human fallibility aside, one may be fairly certain that the real issue, seldom brought to the surface, concerns the meaning of liberty and its place in the hierarchy of values. Also, a distinction should be made between the just use of force and whether its use is *noble*. For example: It is just for the public executioner to execute the convicted murderer, but it is not noble. Similarly, it may have been just for a very large and powerful nation to wage war against a tyrannical yet small and relatively weak nation, but it might not have been noble.[13]

Among men of civility and comprehensive vision, force

is necessarily a last resort for the remedy of political evils. As Aristotle has written: "Those who are pre-eminent in merit would be the most justified in attempting sedition, though they are the last to make the attempt."[14] Hence the phrase in the Declaration, "In every stage of these Oppressions We have Petitioned for Redress in the most humble terms." With life, liberty, and the pursuit of happiness at stake, resort to revolution may be a moral imperative. Still, it is a terrible imperative, however moral. It bears repeating that revolution may liberate not only the nobler but the baser passions of the human heart: patriotism and courage, but also petty and pusillanimous self-seeking; the love of liberty and glory, but also the lust for power and domination. If "all experience hath shown, that mankind are more disposed to suffer, while evils are sufferable, than to right themselves by abolishing the forms to which they are accustomed," it is not simply because the bulk of mankind are lacking in public spiritedness, manliness, or honor (though this is too often the case). Every revolution is a cauldron of fearful uncertainty threatening the replacement of one evil with a still greater evil, one tyranny with an even more heinous tyranny.[15] When revolution becomes a moral imperative, it is not enough for the revolutionary statesman to choose the course of the lesser evil, the choice of ordinary political morality. Such are the sufferings which may attend revolution (the loss of life, which is not mere life but all its powers and potentialities), and such are the evils which revolution may bring in its wake (there is always the chance of failure and of fiercer oppression), that the revolutionary statesman must not only pledge his life, his fortune, and his sacred honor, but he must be capable of creating a new political order of such promising and surpassing goodness as to render even the sufferings of revolution a *moral* imperative. How many good men have the heart—let alone the vision—to undertake so challenging a burden? And how many men of succeeding generations are worthy of passing judgment upon them? Before one passes judgment, he would do well to consider the nature of judgment itself.

What is the nature of the intellectual process which issues in any moral decision and which may, for example, conclude that the use of force is a moral imperative? We are in the domain of moral judgment, which is the determination of the indeterminate. The indeterminate is the way facts stand to moral principles and, conversely, how moral principles stand to facts. Since there is an infinitude of facts associated with any problem or occasion, their selection depends on criteria of relevance. Thus, to justify their decision to "throw off" the British government—necessarily involving moral judgment—the statesmen of the Declaration declared: "let Facts be submitted to a candid world." But as already indicated, those "facts" would not have been selected for emphasis, or would have been devoid of meaning, were it not for the moral principles proclaimed in the preamble. Yet the principles of the preamble are themselves "facts," and were themselves brought forth via selective emphasis. For the truth is there are a multiplicity of moral principles, and which are to be selected for emphasis, or how they are to be ordered, depends on criteria of relevance. Hence the principles are as indeterminate as the "facts." The principles inform the facts, yet the facts elicit the principles. In other words, a reciprocal relation exists between the two, and neither is simply reducible to the other. This runs counter to both empiricism and dogmatism. Facts do *not* speak for themselves in any domain; they do not dictate moral judgment. But neither do moral principles speak for themselves, which is to say that one cannot make moral decisions by descending from general principles to particular facts through deductive logic. Moral judgment is a creative process whereby the individual makes *actual* or determinate certain relationships among the data of experience—and the data include "facts" as well as "principles"—which were *potential* or indeterminate prior to the process.[16]

It follows that there is no essential difference between the process of moral judgment engaged in by the private citizen and that engaged in by the statesman. Indeed, the very dichotomy of private and public, though of great practical importance, is philosophically misleading. The same may be said of the dichotomy of private and public morality. No morality is strictly private in view of the relational essence or mutual immanence of all things. These dichotomies, like that between politics and morality, are all instances of the fallacy of misplaced concreteness. Certainly the Declaration of Independence provides no warrant for a two-standard morality, one governing the relations between individuals, another the relations between states. Thus, in a letter to Madison, Jefferson wrote: "I know but one code of morality for men, whether acting singly or collectively."[17] Of course, there is a profound difference between a moral *code* and what I have described as the process of moral *judgment*. Although moral precepts are involved in moral judgment, they are mediated by the creativity of reason which actually modifies the meaning of such precepts in the process of adjusting them to each other and to particular facts.

That moral judgment is infinitely more complex and creative than the merely literal application of received moral principles is illustrated in *Federalist* 14, where Madison declares:

> Hearken not to the voice which petulantly tells you that the form of government recommended for your adoption is a novelty in the political world; that it has never yet had a place in the theories of the wildest projectors. . . . But why is the experiment of an extended republic to be rejected, merely because it may comprise what is new?

And then the sequel cited earlier:

> Is it not the glory of the people of America, that, whilst they have

paid a decent regard to the opinions of former times . . . they
have not suffered a blind veneration for antiquity . . . to overrule the suggestions of their own good sense, the knowledge of
their own situation, and the lessons of their own experience?[18]

The data of their experience did not—and alone could not—
impose upon the founders the idea of an extended republic.
Those data consisted of a welter of "facts" among which
were (1) countless "defects" of government under the
Articles of Confederation (elaborated throughout *The
Federalist*), which were defects, however, only in virtue of
the political standards or goals of the founders; (2) the
political, moral, and religious similarities of the American
people (emphasized in *Federalist* 2), which were politically
more significant than their dissimilarities only in virtue of
the founders' own criteria of relevance; and (3) the sheer
vastness of the American continent, itself politically
meaningless unless conjoined with the "facts" already
mentioned. It was the creative reason of the founders and
their idea of an extended republic (itself a synthesis of an
incredible number of moral judgments) that endowed the
facts with meaning, made the potential actual, and created
a government which then was, and perhaps still is, "a
novelty in the political world."

This excursus by way of *The Federalist* is intended to
illustrate the complex nature of moral judgment. Its ulterior
purpose is to prepare for one of the most difficult problems
of the Declaration of Independence, namely this: *Who* is
to judge whether any established government has become
destructive of the ends for which government is established,
and therefore, whether it should be abolished or overthrown?
In other words, who is to judge whether revolution has
become a moral imperative?[19] The question may be answered
by elimination.

Since the question presupposes a distinction between the
legal and the just, those who deny this distinction disqualify

themselves from judging whether any revolution is justified. The Declaration, recall, is addressed to "candid" men, men free from the prejudice which identifies the legal and the just, men who know that over and above the laws of parliaments and kings are the laws of nature and of nature's God. These men alone are capable of *moral* judgment. Sad to say, but the Declaration seems to eliminate a very large portion of mankind, learned as well as ignorant, from judging whether it is ever right to violate the laws of one's country, hence from judging the statesmen of the Declaration. Perhaps this is one reason why those statesmen do not appeal to "World Opinion" or to "History," but rather to God for the rectitude of their intentions, although the issue here concerns not their intentions but their judgment. Be this as it may, the question remains, who is to judge whether revolution is a moral imperative?

The obvious answer would appear to be the people. Does not the Declaration say it is the "Right of the People to alter or to abolish" their government should it become destructive of the ends for which government is established, and then "to institute new Government, laying its foundation on such principles and organizing its powers in such form as *to them* shall seem most likely to effect their Safety and Happiness?" (italics added). Having the right to abolish an unjust government, the people may be presumed capable of judging whether their government deserves to be abolished. The right itself presupposes this capacity, and it cannot properly be exercised without it. This conforms to the position taken earlier on the question, *What kind of being is man such that he, unlike all other creatures, should be endowed with the rights to life, liberty, and the pursuit of happiness?* What renders men worthy of those rights, we saw, are their intellectual and moral endowments. Applied to the point at issue, it is the critical and constructive intellect, together with the considerateness of civility, that enables men to judge rightly when to abolish an unjust government and how to design a new one more conducive to their safety and happiness.

We have seen, however, that according to the very standards implicit in the Declaration, a large portion of mankind is not qualified to render the judgment in question, especially in view of the complex nature of moral judgment. Does the Declaration, therefore, contradict itself when it proclaims the right of the people to overthrow a government when it has violated the ends for which it was established? Not at all. The Declaration was not written for thoughtless and intemperate men. Those who signed that document had a profound respect for reason as well as an abiding concern for justice. Under the circumstances, they necessarily emphasized men's natural rights, including the right of revolution. But men have no natural right to act foolishly or unjustly. As Jefferson himself has written: "I am convinced man has no natural right in opposition to his social duties," and that "questions of natural right are triable by their conformity with the moral sense and reason of man."[20] And as we have seen in the Declaration, "Prudence, indeed, will dictate that Governments long established should not be changed for light and transient causes." On the other hand, it must be admitted that while Jefferson was in Paris, he did write—in private correspondence to be sure—that "a little rebellion now and then is a good thing," in fact, that "The tree of liberty must be refreshed from time to time with the blood of patriots and tyrants. It is its natural manure."[21] (No sentimental humanitarian was the sage of Monticello who compared the blood of patriots with dung!) Though prudence will dictate that governments long established should not be changed for light and transient causes, still it is the right of the people to be the judges of what is "light" and "transient." And to the support of this contention one may refer to Jefferson's reputed confidence in the people. What is usually forgotten, however, is that Jefferson placed his confidence in an agrarian people who possessed their own land and who were therefore independent and self-reliant. Such a people, he felt, would not easily be swayed by demagogues or by light and transient causes. Furthermore, Jefferson's confidence in the people extended little further than their ability to participate in local government (for the most part at the ward level) and to choose representatives for the more extensive and complex affairs of the national government. Admittedly, he did indeed believe that the yeomanry were good judges of character and, given their independence, could usually be depended upon to elect men of wisdom and virtue.[22] But note well this passage from one of Jefferson's celebrated letters to John Adams:

> I agree with you that there is a natural aristocracy among men. The grounds of this are virtue and talents. . . . The natural aristocracy I consider as the most precious gift of nature for the instruction, the trusts, and government of society. . . . May we not even say that that form of government is the best which provides the most effectually for a pure selection of these natural *aristoi* into the offices of government?[23]

It was precisely to facilitate the selection of the natural *aristoi*—the genuine elited—that Jefferson again and again emphasized the importance of educating the people and of fostering a way of life conducive to the development of a virtuous and deferential citizenry. Had he harbored a naive trust in the people he would not have been so concerned to instruct them. The truth is that Jefferson was more than skeptical about "the people"; he seriously doubted whether the patriotism and love of liberty they displayed during the Revolution would long endure—and this is precisely why he believed that "a little rebellion now and then is a good thing."[24]

But still, who is to initiate this "little rebellion" which Jefferson believed is the only way of rekindling among the people the patriotism and love of liberty displayed during the Revolution? Obviously not the people themselves who "are more disposed to suffer, while evils are sufferable, than to right themselves by abolishing the forms to which they are accustomed." No, should government become destructive of their rights it will not be "the people" who will first feel the yoke of tyranny descending upon them. Rather, it will be the natural *aristoi*, endowed by nature with critical and constructive intellect, who will first discern the signs of tyranny, men whose sense of honor will not permit them to suffer indefinitely the evils and indignities of despotism. I call such men philosophic statesmen. They alone can judge when revolution becomes a *moral* imperative. For only those who can create the new can judge rightly when to destroy the old.*

Having said this, however, I must now qualify the argument by recalling the architectonic principle of the Declaration and elaborating on its revolutionary significance.

Because the Declaration is based on the primacy of reason, and because reason is available in principle to all mankind, the government envisioned by the statesmen of the American Revolution would have, as its highest end, the education of an enlightened body of citizens. "The culti-

---

*I have been making an implicit distinction between the exoteric and esoteric teachings of the Declaration concerning revolution. That the people have a right to abolish unjust government and institute a new government conducive to their safety and happiness is positively asserted. Notice, however, that the assertion is made by the *representatives* of the people, I mean by those who signed the Declaration. In principle, such representatives would consist of Jefferson's natural *aristoi*, with the implication that the people would be sufficiently enlightened to select *aristoi* as their representatives. Now, because the rights proclaimed by the Declaration are self-evident, the people, being enlightened, are capable of recognizing their violation by government (which is why they are moved to rebel in the first place). But only the *aristoi* know how to articulate those rights and how to apply them judiciously in the construction of a new government. We thus see in the Declaration a mixture or synthesis of democratic and aristocratic principles, anticipating the "mixed regime" reflected in the American Constitution.

vation and improvement of the human mind," said James Wilson at the Constitutional Convention, "[is] the most noble object [of government]."[25] And Jefferson said: "I look to the diffusion of light and education as the resource to be relied on for . . . promoting the virtue and advancing the happiness of man."[26] This intention, of educating the people to the heights of self-government, *without in the meantime postponing the principle of government by the consent of the governed*, is the most revolutionary implication of the Declaration of Independence (even though a fairly enlightened people is presupposed to begin with). This is what makes the American Revolution the revolution *par excellence*. In comparison, the Bolshevik Revolution, like Communist revolutions in general, was reactionary. For that revolution ushered in a form of government whose rulers, in the name of the proletariat, have shown nothing but contempt for their own people during the past six decades, having suppressed their liberty and deluged them with the crudest mendacity. Here we see the profound difference between a revolution based on the primacy of force and one based on the primacy of reason. Only the latter is truly revolutionary.

Five On Equality and Self-Determination

That all men are born to equal rights is true. Every being has a right
to his own, as clear, as moral, as sacred as any other being has. This is
as indubitable as a moral government in the universe. But to teach
that all men are born with equal powers and faculties, to equal
influence in society, to equal property and advantages through life,
is as gross a fraud, as glaring an imposition on the credulity of the
people as ever was practiced by monks . . . by Brahmins . . . or
by the self-styled philosophers of the French revolution. For honor's
sake . . . for truth and virtue's sake, let American philosophers
and politicians despise it. | John Adams
How insipidly uniform would human life and manners be, without
the beautiful variety of colours, reflected upon them by different
tastes, different tempers, and different characters! | James Wilson

IT was precisely in the act of destroying the old and
creating the new that a people became the American
people; for it was then that they achieved that high
tension of public spiritedness, that dedication to the common good which is patriotism. But the revolutionary
statesmen of the Declaration were the ones who called the
American people into being, who laid down the law of their
future development, and who endowed them with a universal mission. This was the work of true individuality which,
by the power of the metaphysical reason, transcends time
and space. This was the work of true liberty which, by the
discipline of the pragmatic reason, only flourishes in the
effectiveness of purpose. But what of true equality?

When I behold the face of another man, a stranger, I
know that he is a *human* being, that he and I are members
of the same species, despite differences in our physical
appearance. To be sure, I would not know that we belong
to the same species were it not for the similarity of our

appearance. But this visible similarity serves only to evoke the awareness of things non-visible. Beholding his face I know, for example, that he, like me, has need for food and drink. Since these needs are not peculiar to human beings, however, they cannot of themselves evoke the awareness that we are members of the same species. If I now ask, in virtue of what is our shared humanity evident? I answer, in virtue of an awareness of something not visible in each of us that renders it impossible for either of us wholly to belong to the other. That something is the *different sameness* of human individuality apprehended by the differentiating and assimilative power of reason. Possessed of that power, I know that the stranger whose face I am looking at is his own center of purposes, purposes which may more or less coincide (but never entirely) with my own. In this context, reason may be regarded as the power of individuality extending its character into its environment and selectively assimilating its environment into itself. Thus could the authors of the Declaration "assume among the powers of the earth, the separate and equal station to which the Laws of Nature and of Nature's God entitle them." Thus could they proclaim that all men are created equal, equal in the sense of being endowed by their Creator with those unalienable rights to life, liberty, and the pursuit of happiness.[1]

And yet, however self-evident the truth that all men are created equal, we know beyond a doubt that such is the dispensation of nature and of nature's God that men are born unequal in their intellectual, moral, and physical endowments. Not only is there a hierarchy in the universe extending through beast and man to God, but there is also a hierarchy among men themselves. To some this may be the cause for bitter resentment. To others it is the precondition of magnanimity, of all excellence and greatness. Still, the Declaration emphasizes equality, not inequality. Could it be that that equality is a precondition for true individuality, for true liberty, and for the ascendency of reason in political life? Is it possible, therefore, that the equality of which the Declaration speaks is a precondition for the rule of a natural *aristoi?* I shall argue that this is precisely the case, that the Declaration embodies the possibility of a semi-aristocratic political philosophy consistent with its basically aristocratic conception of human nature.

When the statesmen of the Declaration proclaim that all men are created equal, they are informing mankind in general, but the British government in particular, that the American people belong to the same species as the English people, *homo rationalis et civilis*, hence that they have been endowed with the natural rights peculiar to that species. Their complaint was that while they possess those rights *qua species*, they were being unjustly prevented from fully exercising those rights *qua individuals*. This implicit distinction between the *possession* and the *exercise* of rights is profound.

From a larger perspective, nothing in the Declaration suggests that *all* men as *individuals* are entitled to the actual *exercise* of their natural rights without qualification. In virtual proof of this it is sufficient to point out that not only was the preamble of the Declaration (or its equivalent) incorporated into most of the state constitutions, but many of these constitutions prescribed property and other qualifications for voting and for holding office. (This fact alone seriously weakens the long-standing interpretation of the Constitution as a "conservative reaction" to the supposedly democratic principles of the Declaration.) Men do indeed possess certain natural rights, but the particular manner of their enjoyment is a subject to be determined by law, either customary or statute. Even had the Declaration claimed that all men possess a natural right to vote or to hold office, still there would remain the question of *how* these rights ought to be exercised, and property or other qualifications would not be logically excluded. In fact, however, the right to vote or to hold office is not a *self-evident* truth and cannot be inferred from one. In other words, the inferred truth that government rests on the consent of the governed does not entail unqualified universal suffrage. Besides, the principle of consent includes tacit as well as expressed consent, as the phrase "whenever *any* Form of Government becomes destructive of [men's natural rights]" clearly indicates. Even the most democratic of governments rests largely on tacit consent, and could not otherwise function given the countless and urgent political decisions which must be made without recourse to the governed.[2] But the point to bear in mind is that there is nothing inconsistent between the notion of government based on the consent of the governed and the institution of property and other qualifications for voting and for holding office.

To avoid democratic doctrinairism, the meaning of consent should not be torn from the context of the Declaration and translated simply into a voluntaristic concept. The Declaration, we have seen, enthrones reason as the architectonic principle of political rule. Precisely because man is *homo rationalis et civilis*, he may not be ruled without his consent. Consent must therefore be assimilated to the metaphysical reason (with the help of the pragmatic reason as I shall soon explain). Think of a person reaching the "age of consent" or the "age of discretion."[3] He is presumed to have achieved a certain degree of intellectual independence on the one hand, and a certain degree of civility on the other. He may now be regarded as a moral agent. He is deliberate rather than impulsive. He acts out of motives larger than his immediate pleasure and advantage. He is duly concerned about the good of others, that is, he sees in the good of others his own good. And should he have property of his own, then, as Jefferson understood, this provides a reasonable assurance that, in deliberating on public problems, he will not consent to any unjust deprivation of the property of others.[4] In this light, government based on the explicit consent of the governed (say through the election of representatives) may be regarded as a *method*—the method *par excellence*—of securing men's natural rights. It should be emphasized, however, that the consent method presupposes an enlightened body of citizens and hence is not to be employed indiscriminately among all peoples.

Rooted in *homo rationalis*, the consent method of government requires rational and systematic inquiry, for example, into the qualifications of the representatives. Here is how James Wilson envisioned this process:

> At every important election, a number of important appointments must be made. To do this, is, indeed, the business of a day. But it ought to be the business of much more than a day to be prepared for doing it well. When a citizen elects to office . . . he performs an act of the first political consequence. He should be employed, on every convenient occasion, in making researches after proper persons for filling the different departments of power; in discussing, with his neighbors and fellow citizens, the qualities that should be possessed by those who fill the several offices; and in acquiring information, with the spirit of manly candour, concerning the manners, and history, and characters of those, who are likely to be candidates for the public choice. A habit of conversing and reflecting on these subjects, and of governing his actions by the result of his deliberations, will form, in the mind of the citizen, a uniform, a strong, and a lively sensibility to the interests of his country. . . .
>
> By these means, and in this manner, pure and genuine patriotism —the kind which consists in liberal investigation and disinterested conduct—is produced, cherished, and strengthened. . . .[5]

For this statesman of the Declaration, rational inquiry is almost a spiritual affair, suggestive of the dedication and seriousness of religion. Yet government based on the consent of the governed stands or falls on that kind of inquiry. It presupposes that the conclusions of such inquiry will reflect the enlightened will or the deliberate sense of the community, and that these conclusions will result from "reflection and choice," not from "accident and force."

We can now see more clearly why there is nothing inconsistent between government based on consent and the institution of modest income qualifications for voting and for public office. The institution of such qualifications may be regarded as the conclusion of an inquiry into the most expedient means of ensuring the intellectual and moral integrity of the consent method of government—itself a means, admittedly of a high order, by which to secure the ends of government.

As a method of reaching political decisions, consent substitutes, for the authority of custom and name, the authority of the metaphysical and pragmatic reason. The pragmatic reason examines the patterns and probabilities of human behavior occurring under a variety of circumstances. For example, suppose the population of the country were for the most part living barely above subsistence, but that a politically significant proportion were permanently unemployed welfare recipients. Would it be unjust or unwise to institute a moderate income tax qualification for voting? Indeed, would such a qualification be politically avoidable? Consider. So long as men who labor live in relative comfort, they may not object to sharing the suffrage with the less fortunate, those permanently unemployed recipients of welfare. When, however, those who labor to live from hand to mouth must labor for the unemployed as well, do not expect them long to suffer the principle of "one man, one vote." Sooner or later they or their spokesman will say, with John Stuart Mill, that

> the assembly which votes the taxes . . . should be elected exclusively by those who pay something towards the taxes. Those who pay no taxes, disposing by their votes of other people's money, have every motive to be lavish and none to economise. As far as money matters are concerned, any power of voting possessed

by them is a violation of the fundamental principle of free government; a severance of the power of control from the interest in its beneficial exercise. It amounts to allowing them to put their hands into other people's pockets for any purpose which they think fit to call a public one . . . [6]

This passage recalls one of the cardinal principles of the American Revolution, the principle of "no taxation without representation." For, had the Americans paid no taxes, they could hardly have claimed a right to representation on such matters. But let us go deeper into the rationale for a modest income tax qualification for voting. (I am far from suggesting it would be a just or practical measure under present-day circumstances.*)

Instituting a modest income tax qualification may be regarded as a conclusion (or an inductive generalization) based on data concerning the behaviors of permanently unemployed recipients of public welfare. Analysis of individual instances reveals (so the conclusion implies) that a vast and politically decisive majority of the permanently unemployed will fail to live up to the intellectual and moral standards required for the consent method of government, the rationality of which depends on freedom from compulsion or on intellectual independence. The political judgment of necessitous men is especially susceptible to the influence of demagogues, and from the "right" as well as from the "left." A moderate income tax qualification would render it more difficult for anti-intellectual demagogues of the "right" to inflame the poor against the educated, while making it more difficult for pseudo-intellectuals of the "left" to arouse the poor man's greed called envy. Such a restriction of the suffrage would secure the political power of the

---

*To avoid misunderstanding, I hold that it is right for federal and state governments to facilitate, in various ways, full employment. I also hold that it is the duty of private corporations to cooperate in such endeavors.

middle class and thereby tend to promote certain virtues, especially moderation and deference.[7] These qualities are indispensable for the selection of any natural *aristoi*. Certainly they increase the likelihood that rulers, hence the laws, will be neutral as between the rich and poor. The property of the rich would be protected, but so too would the rights of the poor. Those rights include, of course, the right of *anyone* to vote or hold office upon meeting the requisite qualifications. In other words, any person possessing those qualifications lawfully *merits* the *privilege* of exercising the rights he always possessed *qua* species, but which he may only now exercise *qua* individual.

It follows that whereas the rights men possess *qua* species are defined by nature, the privileges they exercise *qua* individuals are defined by law, whether written or customary. Accordingly, the equality spoken of in the Declaration does not extend to privileges.[8] Nevertheless—and strange as it may seem—the notion of meriting a privilege is a logical consequence of the Declaration's principle of equality. For the truth that all men are created equal constitutes a moral prohibition against any and all privileges based on race, nationality, class, or parentage. The only moral title to any privilege which society may confer must be based on *individual merit*. This means that individual effort is an essential principle of the Declaration's political philosophy. The necessity of individual effort is clearly implied in the affirmation of mankind's right to the *pursuit* of happiness.

At this stage of my argument the reader will not be surprised to learn that, contrary to almost universal opinion, equality of opportunity, which derives from the teaching of the Declaration that all men are created equal, is *not*, teleologically considered, a democratic principle. Equality of opportunity means that no station in life, or no privilege which society may confer, can rightly be denied to any person on grounds other than merit. The rewards of merit constitute advantages not enjoyed by those who have yet to earn them. Those who have yet to earn them are not *dis*advantaged; nor have they been deprived of their rights— as if some malevolent power from without had invaded and emasculated them. They retain the right to earn the privilege earned by others.* This is perfectly in accord with the principle of equality of opportunity, since a person's opportunities in life depend not only on external circumstances, but on his own intellectual and moral qualities as well. Some people make their opportunities, or the best of their talents, and circumstances. Some do not.

From this teleological perspective, equality of opportunity is an aristocratic principle. It encourages the thrust of individuality in its quest for self-transcendence. It sustains liberty in the quest for effectiveness of purpose. And because it promises the rewards of merit, it energizes the pursuit of happiness.

Now to grasp the deeper significance of the principle of equality, I shall examine two key passages of the Declaration of Independence of the so-called Democratic Republic of Vietnam promulgated by Ho Chi Minh in 1945.

The preamble of that Marxist declaration begins with the words of the American Declaration, namely: "All men are created equal. They are endowed by their Creator with certain unalienable rights, among these are Life, Liberty and the pursuit of Happiness." After crediting the original, the document goes on to explain: "In a broader sense, this means: 'All the peoples on earth are equal from birth, all the peoples have a right to live, be happy and free.'" Having so ingenuously transformed *men's* unalienable right to *pursue* happiness into the right of all *peoples* to *be happy*— thereby suppressing the implicit notion of individual effort, hence of freedom and responsibility—logical as well as moral

*To be sure, many of the privileged have not earned their privileges. However, as a result of inverse discrimination, we may now include among the privileged some of the so-called underprivileged.

consistency required the author or authors to transform the peroration of the American Declaration from *"we* [the signatories of this Declaration] pledge *to each other our* Lives, *our* Fortunes and *our* sacred Honor" into: "The entire Vietnamese people are determined to mobilize all *their* physical and mental strength, to sacrifice *their* lives and property in order to safeguard *their* independence and liberty" (italics added in both quotations).[9] Conspicuously missing here is the word *honor*—an aristocratic motif foreign to Marxist thought and temperament. For honor, as the correlate of the sense of shame, involves a power within the individual over himself and over external circumstances. This power, we have seen, has its origin in the metaphysical reason on which morality and religion depend. But Marxism regards metaphysics, like morality and religion, as a "phantom" of the brain, the "reflex" of material or economic premises. With behaviorism, Marxism reduces and degrades human thought or reason to the pragmatic level of an instrument, the instrument of material interests. By denying to reason any initiatory power, that is, by denying any semblance of intellectual independence, Marxism strips the individual of political independence as well. The individual is simply a member of a class: his thoughts—such as those concerning right and wrong—are the thoughts of his class and merely serve his class interests. His morality is class morality. Applying this teaching to the accomplishments of the individual in any domain of thought, it follows that his intellectual accomplishments are in fact reflections of the mentality of his class. It would be erroneous, therefore, to praise or reward him on the basis of individual merit, since intellectual achievement is the product of man *qua* species, rather than of man *qua* individual—only now there are as many species as there are classes. Thus, by stripping the individual of any intellectual independence, Marxism strips him of his dignity, his honor.

Having seen in the Ho Chi Minh Declaration of Independence an implicit denial of individual effort, freedom, and responsibility on the one hand, and a profound silence regarding personal honor on the other—a denial and silence intimately related to the avowed right of all peoples to be happy—how might one account for the virtual repudiation of that right by the statesmen of the American Declaration of Independence? Perhaps the explanation ultimately derives from the classical-*cum*-Christian recognition of human imperfection. Simply stated, because men are not all wise and virtuous, they cannot reasonably claim a right to *be* happy, although they may certainly claim a right to *pursue* happiness. And their happiness would require their striving toward perfection *qua* species to be modulated by their perfection *qua* individuals. Now if imperfection is, as the Great Tradition maintained, an ineluctable, albeit mitigable, fact of nature (on which, incidentally, both tragedy and comedy are based), then the denial of imperfection, or the belief that it can be overcome by socio-economic or other means, would encourage if not justify tyranny.* For involved in the denial of human imperfection is a rejection of the classical and biblical understanding that man's nature, being immutable, will ever be subject to such faults and vices as ignorance and insincerity, conceit and self-indulgence, envy and irascibility, all of which may be mitigated but never entirely eradicated by human institutions. Rejected, in other words, is the view that to be human is to have beast-like as well as God-like qualities, qualities which endow man with the freedom to live in accordance with what is beneath him or in accordance with what is above him.

The denial that man's nature is immutable, and the related denial of a hierarchical universe in which man is

---

*If self-consistent, the recognition of human imperfection will foster modesty and moderation, rendering men more tolerant of human frailty and less resentful of adversity. To that extent it will militate against utopianism as well as political fanaticism.

between beast and God, may help to explain why the Marxist Declaration of Ho Chi Minh asserts that all *peoples* are equal (and have a right to be happy). For that two-fold denial entails the negation of any universal and trans-historical standard of perfection in terms of which one could determine the level to which any people, by virtue of their strivings and intellectual, political, economic, and artistic accomplishments, were worthy of emulation and honor. Marxist equality thus tends to dissolve the distinctions among men: the distinction between the competent and incompetent, the temperate and the intemperate, the diligent and the indolent, the refined and the crude. Regardless of these distinctions, all peoples (but therefore all groups composing a particular society) would have a right to be happy.[10] This levelling equality stands in the sharpest contrast with the equality intrinsic to the American Declaration of Independence. Teleologically considered, and again as suggested by the very notion of the *pursuit* of happiness, the equality proclaimed by the statesmen of the American Declaration is to be understood as the reward of striving toward some humane goal or excellence. In the American founding, therefore, equality was intended to be an *elevating* principle of political life. This was clearly understood by Andrew Johnson:

> I believe man can be elevated; man can become more and more endowed with divinity; and as he does he becomes more God-like in his character and capable of governing himself. Let us go on elevating our people, perfecting our institutions, until democracy shall reach such a point of perfection that we can acclaim with truth that the voice of the people is the voice of God.[11]

Notice that the regime here described as democratic could more accurately be described as a universal aristocracy or as an aristocratic democracy. Whichever the case, these few lines lend support to a semi-aristocratic interpretation of the Declaration of Independence. Merely by juxtaposing those lines with the phrase "all men are created equal," it becomes evident that the equality of all men consists in their participation in the divine nature. And insofar as those lines give voice to the silence of the Declaration, it may also be said that the paramount purpose of political institutions is to facilitate the cultivation of the divine nature in man such that his pursuit of happiness will in truth be the striving toward perfection.

From the truth that all men are created equal, which affirms that all men belong to the species *homo rationalis*, creatures capable of reflection and choice, there follows the political principle of self-determination. I say "political" because it happens to be the case that self-determination has a biological foundation in the organic and teleological understanding of life, which holds that all living things possess an internal principle of motion and *purposive* change. To say that a living thing is self-determinative is to say that its behavior is not simply the resultant of external forces; that these forces only modulate the internal thrust of the organism which is to reach the completion of its self-development. Were it not for the fact that each organism has an internal principle of motion and change tending toward the completion of its own nature, or conversely, if the behavior of all living things was merely the resultant of external forces, then it would be difficult indeed to account for the existence of so many species each with its own enduring form. In any case, it is precisely because each organism has an internal principle of motion and change that we have, as humans, the notion of individual responsibility. (This is one reason why self-determination is a moral principle.) On the other hand, because external forces influence the growth of any organism—the environment can be conducive as well as unconducive to its self-realization—there also obtains the notion of social responsibility. The environment obviously includes other individuals. It may be said, therefore, that just as the environment enters into the character of each individual, so each individual extends its character into the environment (a point made earlier). From this reciprocal relationship between individual and environment is derived the notion of rights and corresponding duties. This is what lies behind Jefferson's remark that "man has no natural right in opposition to his social duties" —a conclusion which may be drawn collaterally from the premise that all men are created equal or equally belong to the same species.

It follows that the meaning of self-determination should not be simply opposed to sociological determination. The self is not hermetically sealed. Nor is it a tabula rasa, a passive lump of clay. There is a reciprocal relationship between individual and environment, but the self does not passively receive the influences streaming into it from society. There is discrimination, amplification, and attenuation, all of which vary from one individual to another. And it is not very helpful to add that the process of selection is traceable to the antecedents of the individual, for they too are subject to selective emphasis. What I am advancing is the notion of an irreducible individuality which is nevertheless organically related to the whole. No two entities can be identical—and this is true of two electrons as well as of two "identical" twins, if only because they occupy different space-time coordinates. Here we again come across the *different sameness* of members of the same species. Among men, this different sameness may be politically translated into a doctrine of *unequal equality*, a doctrine which ultimately derives from the unique relationship of each individual to his Creator. But this touches upon the deepest silence of the Declaration of Independence.* Let us come back a step.

*Although deism or an impersonal deity may be implied in the preamble's "Nature's God," the peroration's appeal to the "Supreme Judge of the world for the rectitude of our intentions" points to a theistic or personal God.

Had the statesmen of the Declaration proclaimed that all men are created unequal, they would have uttered a truth known to virtually everyone, or at least a truth of which few had then to be reminded. The Declaration is a political document; and such were the circumstances of the times that it was infinitely more important to emphasize the seemingly contradictory truth that all men are created equal, a truth which wise and virtuous men will want to uphold as a barrier against tyranny. Accordingly, nothing is more dangerous than to proclaim that all men are created unequal, a truth likely to arm the wicked who, unlike the wise and the virtuous, may be animated by a lust for power and dominion. So, let us say that the Declaration utters a half-truth in proclaiming that all men are created equal; just as it would be a half-truth to say that all men are created unequal. These two truths complete each other and, in so doing, make distributive justice among men possible.

Now, it is precisely the doctrine of unequal equality that makes self-determination a moral—perhaps a cosmic— imperative. Let us look about us. We see a multiplicity of different things. While some things obstruct each other, others cooperate and intensify each other. As a matter of fact, even the mutual obstruction of things can engender cooperation and mutual intensification. In other words, this universe in which we find ourselves is a vast, complex network of interdependency. From the perspective of the whole, many finite evils, which we are morally obliged to fight, may be regarded as contributing to the good of the whole. But what has all this to do with self-determination? Simply this. On the one hand, if natural inequality is to contribute to the good of the whole, each individual must have the opportunity to develop his own particular excellence. On the other hand, if natural equality is to contribute to the good of the whole, the development of each individual's particular excellence must be assimilated to, and inevitably modified by, the particular excellences of the

other individuals composing his society. Uncoordinated
particularity is self-defeating, which is to say that coordination is essential to the realization of the diverse aims and
interests of men. Inequality is the foundation of pluralism.
It is the precondition of all excellence. But inequality also
results in the mutual obstruction of all good things (which is
one aspect of evil).[12] What saves inequality is its opposite,
equality. Equality insists that each individual has some good
to contribute to the whole. This is why he has the unalienable rights to life, liberty, and the pursuit of happiness. As a
consequence, equality makes possible—and we are obliged
to pursue this possibility—the mutual intensification of all
good things. The degradation of equality is egalitarianism.
Egalitarianism makes equality a levelling principle. It seeks
to dissolve the differences among men. Animated by envy
and resentment, egalitarianism commits the crime of aristo-
cide. Equality, the equality of the Declaration, is of another
order. It is a deferential and elevating principle. It acknowl-
edges excellences in all callings of life. It only insists on
their interdependence. It wishes to remind us that the
higher is dependent on the lower, just as inequality wishes
to remind us that the lower is dependent on the higher.*
What saves equality, therefore, is its opposite, inequality.
Truly, they complete each other.

Inequality makes individuality possible, but therefore
conflict and the need for coercion. Equality makes society
possible, therefore the blessings of friendship and moral
suasion. No one will deny that great individuals are not
possible without society. And surely no society ever achieved
greatness without great individuals. This, too, is why self-
determination is a moral imperative.

It is more than that. Self-determination is a *sine qua non*
of human dignity. Clearly, human dignity stands or falls on
whether the individual possesses freedom, the power to act

---

*But insofar as men are deferential and partake of the divine nature,
the converse of this statement is also true.

according to insight or knowledge as opposed to mere impulse or received opinion. This is why we cherish liberty. Earlier I said that liberty is not an end in itself but a means to a higher end, namely, happiness. Rather than use the terms freedom and liberty interchangeably, as is often done, I shall make the following distinction. Men need not claim a right to freedom because they are free to begin with. But it is precisely because they are free to begin with that they may claim a right to liberty—meaning *political* liberty. Since men are capable of self-determination, they may be held individually (as well as collectively) responsible for their conduct. An individual may therefore be praised or blamed, admired or despised.[13] Conversely, if men are not free, are incapable of self-determination, then, as already suggested, they cannot be held individually (or collectively) responsible for their conduct. Neither praise nor blame, admiration nor contempt would any longer be warranted. The denial of self-determination requires the denial of human dignity and shame.[14] Dissolved in the process is that hierarchy of beast, man, and God. What will take its place? What will take the place of that teaching of the Declaration obscured by the encrusted dogmas of egalitarianism?

However obvious it may now seem in the saying, it none-theless needs to be said that the principles of the Declaration of Independence, especially those concerning liberty and self-determinaton, are utterly contradicted by determinism in general, and by the principles of the behavioral sciences in particular. We have already explored some of the roots of behaviorism in Hobbes who, by rejecting the teleological and hierarchical conception of nature, lowered man to a level little above the beasts. Instead of being the beast with red cheeks, man becomes, in Hobbes and in behaviorism generally, the beast with technique. Again, reason is nothing more than the instrument of men's appetites. No longer is it constitutive of human aims or purposes. Indeed, behavioral scientists reject the very notion of purposiveness in nature, which occasioned Whitehead's remark: "Scientists animated by the purpose of proving they are purposeless constitute an interesting subject for study."[15] Behaviorists tell us that the purposes men pursue are not determined by any instinctive inclinations (such as a natural desire for society or for knowledge), nor by any fusion of reason and will. Men establish governments; but the ends or purposes of government have no sanction in a rational or moral law. And as for the government itself, it does not rest on the *consent* of the governed; for consent is that fusion of reason and will which constitutes the very notion of self-determination rejected by behaviorism.

Strange that a nation whose eighteenth-century colleges and universities educated statesmen dedicated to the establishment of a constitution of government based on "reflection and choice" should in the twentieth century produce countless educators who apparently feel free to teach youth one or another form of determinism, explaining the conduct of men and societies in terms reducible to the play of "accident and force." Meanwhile, other present-day educators apparently feel compelled to propagate the same conclusion from the seemingly opposite doctrine of indeterminism, sometimes called vulgar existentialism. This existentialism (typically, a democratization and misunderstanding of Nietzsche) reaffirms human spontaneity and purposiveness, but contends that human nature is fluid, an ensemble of desires without any fixed purposes or tendencies. These educators acknowledge freedom and self-determination, but this freedom is formless, the product of personal idiosyncracy. Imagine determinists and indeterminists drafting a declaration of *independence* and a constitution of *government*.

Nevertheless, neither school can deny that man is a rational being—rational but also fallible. But what can rationality and fallibility mean to determinists and indeterminists? If reason has no independent agency, and if man has no volition, then it seems rather quaint for a behaviorist to stimulate the public with a theory of human behavior critical of, say, mentalism and then become aroused by the criticism of his own theory. Conversely, if there are no enduring patterns of events to reason about, or if the past is not immanent in the present such as to give some assurance that the future will resemble the past, then it seems very odd indeed for an existentialist to write a book conveying such a teaching with the expectation that its own pattern of meaning will not dissolve before the eyes of his readers.

Apparently, both determinists and indeterminists have exempted themselves from their own conclusions. They have thereby excluded themselves from the human race whose behavior their theories purport to explain. No longer members of the human family, they need feel no moral constraints whatsoever. Each in his own way may then feel perfectly free to create man according to his own personal tastes. Only the product will not be the men of the Declaration. For under the man-made dispensation of determinism-indeterminism (or of behaviorism-existentialism), all "men" will not be created equal, that is, equally endowed by their creators with the unalienable rights to life, liberty, and the pursuit of happiness. Hence they will not possess the right to *self*-determination.

In considering political self-determination, it is commonly overlooked that this principle applies not to the *ends* but to the *forms* of government. The ends are determined by the laws of nature and of nature's God, the forms by men. The ends are general, eternal and immutable. The forms are particular and variable; they depend on the fallible reason of men adapting general ideas to particular facts. All this is true, but too simple.

We have seen that the forms of government are the means which men choose to secure the ends of government. The ends must inform the means, else the means will not be proportioned to the ends. But the ends are general, single terms, and their meaning is not univocal. Notice how the three ends mentioned by the Declaration, life, liberty, and the pursuit of happiness, are of increasing generality, hence of increasing vagueness.[16] Vagueness, however, is not meaninglessness. In fact, every entity is more than it appears to be, since it has significance for an infinitude of entities retreated into the background by its own specious presence. Furthermore, vagueness of ends is a precondition for viable political life. Such vagueness often facilitates cooperation among different men having somewhat divergent interests. The various signatures to the Declaration of Independence confirm this. But what makes the ends of government less vague is, first, their multiplicity and suggestive gradation of rank; second, and more important, the means chosen to achieve these ends. For example, to grasp the meaning of the ends enumerated in the Preamble of the Constitution, it is essential, though admittedly not sufficient, to study the institutional means which the founders designed to achieve those ends. Similarly, to understand the ends of government mentioned in the preamble of the Declaration (especially liberty, which may be translated into self-determination), it is again essential, though not sufficient, to study the catalog of grievances, those "facts" which the statesmen of the Declaration submitted to a "candid world." Let us examine a few of those grievances, and not only for the sake of elucidating the meaning of self-determination, but to see wherein the Declaration anticipates and is completed by the original Constitution.

The first grievance against "the present King of Great Britain" is this: "He has refused his Assent to Laws, the most wholesome and necessary for the public good." The king had an absolute veto over the laws passed by the governments of the several colonies. Responding to the statesmen of the Declaration, the statesmen of the Constitution —six were among both groups—invested the President of the United States with only a qualified or suspensive veto over the laws passed by the national legislature, and none at all over laws enacted by the governments of the several states. Additionally, they decreed that laws must serve the *public* good and not simply some private individual or group. (This, and indeed all the grievances, follows from the principle that all men are created equal.) On the other hand, just as the laws must serve the public good, so individuals and groups are morally obliged to be considerate of the public good when pursuing their own private interests. Here it may be well to point out the error of atomistic individualism and its descendent "group-interest" theory which contend that the public interest is merely the arithmetic sum of the many private interests of the individuals or groups composing a society. This notion is a product of the abstractive intellect and is another instance of misplaced concreteness.[17] Again we may admit an ultimate privacy corresponding to the phenomenon of individuality. But the individual is a center of relationships where the relata enter into his own essence. The individual may thus be regarded as a nucleus of interests, each a quantum of energy modulating the interests of other individuals. This modulation involves amplification and attenuation. Some interests may be compatible and reinforce each other, while others may be incompatible and obstruct each other. The ideal of the laws is to coordinate this welter of interests without losing their vibrant energies—an impossible task, to be sure, but the very lure of architectonic statesmanship. Inevitably, some loss is entailed by any law or public policy. It is not for man or for societies of men to enjoy all good things undiluted. This means that while no law or public policy is perfectly just, neither is any private interest. We are fallible, imperfect beings, whether we are statesmen, businessmen, or educators. All the more reason why no one individual or group should have a monopoly of power. All the more reason why a President should not have an absolute veto over the laws. Although we are fallible, imperfect beings, self-determination is to be cherished, but not as an absolute good.

Here is another grievance against King George III: "He has dissolved Representative Houses repeatedly, for opposing with manly firmness his invasion on the rights of the people." Consistently with the Declaration, the Constitution establishes an independent Congress which cannot be dissolved by the Executive. Note the repeated assumption: since no individual has a monopoly of wisdom and virtue, he ought not to possess a monopoly of power. There is another assumption, namely, that the people are intelligent and deferential enough to appoint intelligent and virtuous men to be their representatives.[18] Again we see that the Declaration is addressed to enlightened men, and that its principles are intended for the governance of an enlightened body of citizens. Only an enlightened people are fully capable of self-determination.

For this reason, the statesmen of the Declaration resented the fact that the King had not only dissolved representative bodies repeatedly, but that "He has refused for a long time, after such dissolutions, to cause others to be elected; whereby the Legislative powers, incapable of Annihilation, have returned to the People at large for their exercise." The statesmen of the Constitution responded by establishing an independent House of Representatives elected by the people every two years, thereby affirming, in a most emphatic way, the principle of government by the consent of the governed, making consent more explicit by the frequency of elections. How else can there be genuine self-determination? It is not enough for an enlightened people to choose statesmen for the purpose of designing a form of government most likely to effect their safety and happiness. Self-determination is not a one-time affair, an election to end all elections. When the Declaration states that men's rights to life, liberty, and the pursuit of happiness are *unalienable*, this means that those rights may neither be taken away *nor voted away*. More, it requires that those elections be genuine, that the public be presented with alternative courses of public policy represented by different candidates for public office. Without denying the importance of institutional forms—for if well-designed they may provide standards for judging the acts of rulers—nevertheless, what is often more decisive is precisely the character of those rulers. Frequently, the forms or institutions of government shape the character of the rulers, the rulers who succeed the founders. (In a free country, this fact should never be forgotten, least of all by political scientists.)[19] Still, in the long run it is the character and aims of those who are elected to office that determine whether the form of government is actually serving the ends for which the government was established. Consequently, if the principle of self-determination is to have on-going efficacy, there must be periodic elections, and the elections must not be the cynical charade typical of certain twentieth-century tyrannies.

The fact that the principle of self-determination necessitates periodic elections, where the people are presented with a choice between candidates having significantly different points of view regarding public policy, recalls the need for civility in public life. One aspect of civility not mentioned earlier is that it disposes men to be friends despite their differences. This touches the deeper meaning of a liberal society. And yet, men cannot truly be friends unless what they have in common is more important than their differences. Lacking this common ground, no society is possible. The Declaration provides such a common ground in its universalist principles, its affirmation of equality and liberty, its respect for reason and truth, to which add the dignity of its language, the moderation of its thought, the manliness of its passion.

It is this common ground that makes periodic elections possible and prevents them from degenerating into civil wars. The candidates confront each other as equals. They are at liberty to speak candidly about public matters: candidly because, while they pay a decent respect to the opinions of mankind, that is, to public opinion, they are men of honor whose first loyalty is to reason and truth. And so the elections follow upon genuine inquiry into what policies will be most conducive to the public good, will best promote private and public happiness. When the elections are over, the contestants, who are of genuinely liberal sentiments, remain friends, or at least do not become enemies. Meanwhile the disappointed portion of the electorate possesses the moderation and manliness to abide by the outcome (and are not animated by rancor or resentment, the easy prey of would-be tyrants). To be sure, it may be said that the disappointed may be kept in good spirit by the prospect of the next election. But this is a narrow and ungenerous point of view. The periodicity of elections itself tends to generate moderation and liberal sentiments, the more so when the victorious are themselves magnanimous. Such, in a word, is the kind of discipline required of a people who wish to enjoy the right to self-determination. That discipline is the epitome of self-determination.

Another significant grievance against the Crown of Great Britain is this: "He has made Judges dependent on his Will alone, for the tenure of their offices." And once again the statesmen of the Constitution responded to the statesmen of the Declaration by establishing an independent judiciary, investing judges of the Supreme Court with a tenure during good behavior, virtually for life.[20] But why so permanent a tenure, especially in view of what has been said about periodic elections and the principle of self-determination? The answer is not complicated. The true ends of government are themselves permanent, while the forms, though subject to change, are relatively permanent in comparison with the policies of government. Regarding the latter, elected officials are necessarily and quite properly concerned with change: how to make things better, and how to prevent things from becoming worse. Hopefully, they will be guided by enduring values, will be able to reconcile permanence and change (one of the most difficult tasks of statesmanship). Elsewhere I have written:

> For it belongs to the goodness of the universe that what men have struggled for and have created in the past should have some relevance for the future. In these terms are we to understand why extraordinary majorities are required to amend the Constitution. . . . That Constitution bears witness to a very simple truth of which statesmen would do well to remind their countrymen, namely, that the living do not possess a monopoly of wisdom. It is a vulgar conceit which violates the reason as well as the goodness of the universe to think that the present, by virtue of . . . evanescent majorities, should possess the power and the right to nullify the works of the past. On the other hand, the same reason and goodness of the universe, again exemplified in the Constitution, denies to the past the power and the right to stifle the creative energies of the present.[21]

The universe requires both permanence and change. To accommodate change there is special need for periodic elections. Those elected necessarily are biased in the direction of change; for there is zest for novelty, for a richer and more comprehensive enjoyment of life's many goods and values. And, too, there is personal ambition, the desire for fame, the urge toward greatness—and so be it. At the same time, however, there is need for permanence without which all is meaningless and vain. Accordingly, there is need for some institution or body of statesmen relatively insulated from the immediate and transient interests of society, men invested with a more or less permanent tenure of office to facilitate not only their independence, but the attainment of judicial wisdom or knowledge concerning the enduring ends of government. Without the equivalent of such an institution, governments would indeed "be changed for light and transient causes." And so here we see, in its permanent judiciary and in its difficult amending process, how the Constitution completes the prudence of the Declaration.*

*In American jurisprudence, a permanent judiciary exercising the power of judicial review is rightly associated with the rule of law. (See *Marbury* v. *Madison*, 1 Cranch 137, 163.) Rooted in the notion of the laws of nature, the rule of law suggests a rational order of things, imbuing mankind with the confidence that the future will resemble the past. (This, incidentally, is the presupposition of inductive logic and of scientific reasoning.) Like the laws of nature, the rule of law precludes sheer arbitrariness. Accordingly, and in contradistinction to the "rule of men," the rule of law restrains or imposes limits on what government may do. Hence the provision in the Constitution for independent courts of justice. As Hamilton points out in *Federalist* 78: "The complete independence of the courts of justice is peculiarly essential in a limited Constitution. By a limited Constitution, I understand one which contains specified exceptions to the legislative authority; such, for instance, as that it shall pass no bills of attainder, no *ex-post-facto* laws, and the like. Limitations of this kind can be preserved in practice no other way than through the medium of courts of justice, whose duty it must be to declare all acts contrary to the manifest tenor of the Constitution void" (505). But while the rule of law restrains government, it also empowers government, enabling it to fulfill its intended purposes. Thus Madison in *Federalist* 51: "In framing a government which is to be administered by men over men, the great difficulty lies in this: you must first enable the government to control the governed, and in the next place oblige it to control itself. A dependence on the people is, no doubt, the primary control on the government; but experience has taught mankind the necessity of auxiliary precautions [such as the system of checks and balances, including the independent courts of justice mentioned by Hamilton]" (337). Furthermore, while the rule of law simultaneously restrains and empowers government, it simultaneously restrains and empowers the governed: for the laws enacted by government, like the laws of nature, embody standards by which to judge and regulate the conduct of men in public as well as in private life. Finally, the rule of law imposes practical restraints on the philosophical intellect, thereby rendering it *more* rational. In its contemplation of perfections, the philosophical intellect may slight the common experience that the ideal is limited by the real, the future by the past. While it is of paramount importance for the philosopher to hold before us the vision of what is noble in thought and in conduct and to remind us of human perfection or greatness, it must also be

There are, of course, other important grievances in the Declaration which find their remedy in the Constitution. The doctrine of civilian supremacy, whereby the President is made the commander-in-chief of the armed forces, responds to the grievance, "He has affected to render the Military independent of and superior to the Civil power." It indicates that the statesmen of the Declaration were committed to a foreign policy of peace rather than of war, that they were more concerned about internal perfection than external glory. But then, any nation dedicated to the principle of self-determination would abhor and vigorously oppose, within the limits of its power, a foreign policy of conquest.

It is worth repeating that self-determination is not a principle to be acted upon solely at the establishment of a government and never thereafter. Men never have a right to act irrationally and unjustly.† Let the electorate of any country vote unanimously in favor of establishing a Communist or a fascist tyranny, that act would not only be irrational—for men cannot rationally divest themselves of the power to determine henceforth who shall be their rulers—but it would also be immoral.

Approaching the problem from another perspective: At

---

borne in mind that the degree to which a people can achieve any perfection will depend on a welter of circumstances: their own intellectual, moral, and material resources; their zest for novelty qualified by their customary ways of thinking and doing things. Here, reason, as already noted, is "the organ of emphasis upon novelty." But the viability of any novel idea in the domain of politics (like the viability of any mutation in the domain of biology) will depend on its capacity to assimilate its environment, which includes the past as it is immanent in the present. The rule of law, which again requires that the future resemble the past, is not a burden imposed on reason's innovations: it is their salvation.

†"[Judge Douglas] contends that whatever community wants slaves has a right to have them. So they have if it is not a wrong. But if it is a wrong, he cannot say any people have a right to do wrong." See Lincoln, *Works*, III, 315.

the end of World War II, it was reasonable and just to impose on Nazi Germany and Imperial Japan a republican form of government, the only form in which the principle of self-determination is meaningful and continuously operative. By means of freedom of speech and press, together with a multiparty system and periodic elections, the people of those two countries now possess, and have for some time exercised, the power to influence public policy and to change the very men responsible for the formulation and execution of public policy. Such self-determination is not to be found among the peoples of Eastern Europe on whom the Soviet Union imposed Communist dictatorships in violation of the Yalta Agreement. The Soviets have gone even further. In the present era of legal realism and political relativism, when democratic statesmen fail to make lucid and educative distinctions between just and unjust forms of government, Communist propaganda has been most effective in using the language of self-determination to thwart the development of this principle in the Third World. I have especially in mind Communist manipulation of so-called national liberation movements in the strategically significant periphery of Asia and Africa—Angola being a Bicentennial example. But the same propaganda or obfuscation is employed by the Soviet-supported Palestine Liberation Organization (the PLO), a terrorist group which, in the name of self-determination, would, if permitted, establish a military dictatorship over the Palestinian people comparable to that of Syria.

Quite clearly there are forms of government which are hostile to the ends of government proclaimed in the Declaration of Independence. This only serves to prove that the forms are not simply neutral vis-à-vis the ends, indeed, that they are themselves articulations and elaborations of the meaning of those ends. This is one reason why it was too simple to say that whereas the ends of government are determined by nature, the forms are determined by man.

Besides, the bifurcation of man and nature is but another instance of the fallacy of misplaced concreteness. Man is part of nature, the part called *human* nature, that part which possesses the greatest freedom or the greatest range of possibilities.[22] Because man's range of possibilities is so vast and indeterminate—no other creature possesses the richness of his imagination, nor the plenitude of his desires —he has been endowed with reason and self-restraint by which to make the possible actual, the indeterminate determinate. By virtue of the discriminating power of reason, man can distinguish between the noble and the base, the just and the unjust, the useful and the harmful; and, assisted as it were by the power of self-restraint, he can choose the former and avoid the latter. Far from being simply a negative force, self-restraint, as previously implied, manifests the power of the individual to coordinate competing aims and interests, subordinating one to another. And since all aims and interests—all possibilities—are in and by themselves mutually exclusive (for each may claim the entire person), *self*-restraint or *self*-control is an absolute precondition for coherent individuality. It is as much a part of nature as self-expression. Actually, it is coterminous with coherent self-expression.[23]

Self-determination may therefore be regarded as a synthesis of self-expression and self-restraint. As such it involves limitations on what any individual or group or nation may do. For example, the principle of self-determination excludes tyranny, for in its own nature tyranny is the unrestrained—unrestrained by the recognition of any law transcending the will of the tyrant. In addition, self-determination excludes the domination by one nation of other nations themselves capable of self-determination. Were this not the case, the principle of self-determination would generate its own contradiction as well as international anarchy.[24]

The particular limits of the principle of self-determination having been stated, a more general limitation needs to be mentioned. Despite the plasticity of human nature, it goes without saying that men are also creatures of habit. We are not simply free to choose our way of life—little more than we are free to choose our parents, the country in which we are born, or the language with which we begin to think and speak. When I said near the outset of this book that what is at once unique and revolutionary about the Declaration is that it inaugurated an era in which governments *might* henceforth be based primarily on rational as opposed to customary foundations, I neglected to point out the obvious, namely, that the rule of reason as a political idea did not originate with the statesmen of the Declaration. The ancestry of that idea goes back to Socrates who, in the *Republic*, establishes a city in which reason is truly sovereign (although only by virtue of a noble lie).[25] Besides, the very effectiveness of reason depends on the development of methods of inquiry and various intellectual skills whose perfection requires not only innovation, but repetition, which is to say custom. And so, self-determination, if it is to be consistent with the Declaration, must preserve the tradition of reason as well as that civility which disposes the mind to the breadth of vision essential to wisdom.

Conclusion

Quite apart from the fact that the term democracy does not appear in the Declaration, we have seen that its underlying conception of human nature is aristocratic, and that its political philosophy includes—I do not say exclusively—aristocratic ideas and values. This is perhaps most evident in the peroration. Listen once more to the words of those statesmen who said, "we mutually pledge to each other our Lives, our Fortunes, and our sacred Honor."

(1) They pledged to each other their *lives:* Life, especially the life of the individual, is of signal importance. Yet the

statesmen of '76 were willing to sacrifice their lives on behalf of the moral and political principles of the Declaration. They did not regard life or mere survival as the highest value.

(2) They pledged to each other their *fortunes*, signifying that private wealth is also important—for which reason economic considerations were a major cause of the American Revolution. And why not? There is a politically decisive connection between economics and independence. Whenever any form of government exercises unqualified control over men's economic activity, the entire range of human freedom is endangered. Private property, though susceptible of abuse by the Few, may also serve to prevent abuses by the One or by the Many. Still, while the statesmen of the Declaration acknowledge the importance of wealth, to call them oligarchs or to regard their revolution simply as bourgeois obscures the palpable truth that the accumulation of riches was not their *summum bonum*.

(3) Finally, the revolutionary statesmen of '76 pledged to each other their sacred *honor*, revealing their aristocratic temperament. The pursuit of wealth without steadfast devotion to just principles they deemed contemptible. This is why the Declaration scorns mercenaries.

These aristocratic dimensions of the Declaration enlarge our moral and intellectual horizons. They recall the passion and civility of men who abhorred not only moral indifference or relativism, but also moral fanaticism or doctrinairism. The mere phrase, "whenever *any* Form of Government becomes destructive of these ends," again, life, liberty and the pursuit of happiness, unambiguously reveals the statesmen's understanding that people of diverse character, customs, and material circumstances require correspondingly diverse forms of government. Nevertheless, to anyone who has not succumbed to the dogma of relativism, this multiplicity of forms inevitably raises the question as to which form of government is the best, that is, which is most conducive to the fullest enjoyment of life, liberty, and the pursuit of happiness. Or in previous terms: Which form of government, above all others, is best designed to bring into coordination the widest range of human values, such that equality dwells with excellence, liberty with virtue, wealth with beauty, the here and now with the eternal? Whatever that form may be, certainly it would not be suitable for all peoples irrespective of their intellectual, moral, and material resources. And to impose such a form on a people ill-equipped to receive it would be tyrannical. Here it may be noted that just as we find within a particular society individuals superior to others in their intellectual and moral endowments, so will we find among different societies one whose way of life is more conducive to the cultivation of those endowments. Certain obscurantists will deny this manifest and unavoidable fact. They would therefore have to reject this statement of John Stuart Mill: "Despotism is a legitimate mode of government in dealing with barbarians, provided the end be their improvement, and the means justified by actually effecting that end."[26]

Still, what form of government is indeed the best? As I have elsewhere written:

> A pluralistic and commercial society ordered by an organic and hierological conception of equality is superior, both in practice *and* in theory, to any classical alternative. Such a society would be highly complex on the one hand, and well-structured on the other. Complexity would facilitate the widest enjoyment of individuality (hence, of freedom). But the effectiveness of individuality, as well as its richness and endurance, requires the rational coordination of contrasting values and relationships; its perfection requires the union of wisdom and virtue. Wisdom and virtue, centered around individuality, would thus remain the cardinal aims of political life.[27]

What I have called "hierological equality" corresponds to the notion of "unequal equality." Thus, while the brain and the heart are equally necessary for the survival of the individual, we nonetheless prefer to live with a weak heart rather than with an infantile brain. Here we see how the hierarchy in the universe is exemplified within a single organism. Indeed, a civilized human being may be regarded as a synthesis of monarchic, aristocratic, and democratic qualities, a synthesis which, writ large, would constitute the very best form of government. In subtle ways such a government was intended by the statesmen of the American Constitution responding to the silence of the Declaration of Independence.[28]

This concludes my attempt to give voice to the silence of certain principles which animated the founders of this Republic. Can American statesmen respond to that silence today? If not, do we have the time to cultivate such statesmen?

Appendix   The Declaration of Independence
In Congress, July 4, 1776
The Unanimous Declaration of the Thirteen
United States of America

W HEN in the Course of human events, it becomes necessary for one people to dissolve the political bands which have connected them with another, and to assume among the powers of the earth, the separate and equal station to which the Laws of Nature and of Nature's God entitle them, a decent respect to the opinions of mankind requires that they should declare the causes which impel them to the separation. We hold these truths to be self-evident, that all men are created equal, that they are endowed by their Creator with certain unalienable Rights, that among these are Life, Liberty and the pursuit of Happiness.—That to secure these rights, Governments are instituted among Men, deriving their just powers from the consent of the governed.—That whenever any Form of Government becomes destructive of these ends, it is the Right of the People to alter or to abolish it, and to institute new Government, laying its foundation on such principles and organizing its powers in such form, as to them shall seem most likely to effect their Safety and Happiness. Prudence, indeed, will dictate that Governments long established should not be changed for light and transient causes; and accordingly all experience hath shown, that mankind are more disposed to suffer, while evils are sufferable, than to right themselves by abolishing the forms to which they are accustomed. But when a long train of abuses and usurpations, pursuing invariably the same Object evinces a design to reduce them under absolute Despotism, it is their right, it is their duty, to throw off such Government, and to provide new Guards for their future security.—Such has been the patient sufferance of these Colonies; and such is now the necessity which constrains them to alter their former Systems of Government. The history of the present King of Great Britain is a history of repeated injuries and usurpations, all having in direct object the establishment of an absolute Tyranny over these States. To prove this, let Facts be submitted to a candid world.—He has refused his Assent to Laws, the most wholesome and necessary for the public good.—He has forbidden his Governors to pass Laws of immediate and pressing importance, unless suspended in their operation till his Assent should be obtained; and when so suspended, he has utterly neglected to attend to them.— He has refused to pass other Laws for the accommodation of large districts of people, unless those people would relinquish the right of Representation in the Legislature, a right inestimable to them and formidable to tyrants only.— He has called together legislative bodies at places unusual, uncomfortable, and distant from the depository of their public Records, for the sole purpose of fatiguing them into compliance with his measures.—He has dissolved Representative Houses repeatedly, for opposing with manly firmness his invasions on the rights of the people.—He has refused for a long time, after such dissolutions, to cause others to be elected; whereby the Legislative powers, incapable of Annihilation, have returned to the People at large for their exercise; the State remaining in the mean time exposed to all the dangers of invasion from without, and convulsions within.—He has endeavoured to prevent the population of these States; for that purpose obstructing the Laws for Naturalization of Foreigners; refusing to pass others to encourage their migration hither, and raising the conditions of new Appropriations of Lands.—He has obstructed the Administration of Justice, by refusing his Assent to Laws for establishing Judiciary powers.—He has made Judges dependent on his Will alone, for the tenure of their offices, and the amount and payment of their salaries.—He has erected a multitude of New Offices, and sent hither swarms of Officers to harrass our people, and eat out their substance.—He has kept among us, in times of peace, Standing Armies, without the Consent of our legislatures.—He has affected to render the Military independent of and superior to the Civil power.—He has combined with others to subject us to a jurisdiction foreign to our constitution, and unacknowledged by our laws; giving his Assent to their Acts of pretended Legislation:—For quartering large bodies of armed troops among us:—For protecting them, by a mock Trial, from punishment for any Murders which they should commit on the Inhabitants of these States:—For cutting off our Trade with all parts of the world:—For imposing Taxes on us without our Consent:—For depriving us in many cases, of the benefits of Trial by Jury:—For transporting us beyond Seas to be tried for pretended offences:—For abolishing the free System of English Laws in a neighbouring Province, establishing therein an Arbitrary government, and enlarging its Boundaries so as to render it at once an example and fit instrument for introducing the same absolute rule into these Colonies:—For taking away our Charters, abolishing our most valuable Laws, and altering fundamentally the Forms of our Governments:—For suspending our own Legislatures, and declaring themselves invested with power to legislate for us in all cases whatsoever. —He has abdicated Government here, by declaring us out of his Protection and waging War against us.—He has plundered our seas, ravaged our Coasts, burnt our towns, and destroyed the lives of our people.—He is at this time transporting large Armies of foreign Mercenaries to complete the works of death, desolation and tyranny, already begun with circumstances of Cruelty & perfidy scarcely paralleled in the most barbarous ages, and totally unworthy the Head of a civilized nation.—He has constrained our fellow Citizens taken Captive on the high Seas to bear Arms against their

Country, to become the executioners of their friends and Brethren, or to fall themselves by their Hands.—He has excited domestic insurrections amongst us, and has endeavoured to bring on the inhabitants of our frontiers, the merciless Indian Savages, whose known rule of warfare, is an undistinguished destruction of all ages, sexes and conditions. In every stage of these Oppressions We have Petitioned for Redress in the most humble terms: Our repeated Petitions have been answered only by repeated injury. A Prince, whose character is thus marked by every act which may define a Tyrant, is unfit to be the ruler of a free people. Nor have We been wanting in attentions to our British brethren. We have warned them from time to time of attempts by their legislature to extend an unwarrantable jurisdiction over us. We have reminded them of the circumstances of our emigration and settlement here. We have appealed to their native justice and magnanimity, and we have conjured them by the ties of our common kindred to disavow these usurpations, which, would inevitably interrupt our connections and correspondence. They, too, have been deaf to the voice of justice and of consanguinity. We must, therefore, acquiesce in the necessity, which denounces our Separation, and hold them, as we hold the rest of mankind, Enemies in War, in Peace Friends.—

We, therefore, the representatives of the United States of America, in General Congress, Assembled, appealing to the Supreme Judge of the world for the rectitude of our intentions, do, in the Name, and by the Authority of the good People of these Colonies, solemnly publish and declare, That these United Colonies are, and of Right ought to be free and independent states; that they are Absolved from all Allegiance to the British Crown, and that all political connection between them and the State of Great Britain, is and ought to be totally dissolved; and that as Free and Independent States, they have full Power to levy War, conclude Peace, contract Alliances, establish

Commerce, and to do all other Acts and Things which Independent States may of right do.—And for the support of this Declaration, with a firm reliance on the protection of Divine Providence, we mutually pledge to each other our Lives, our Fortunes and our sacred Honor.

John Hancock

New Hampshire
Josiah Bartlett,
Wm. Whipple,
Matthew Thornton.

Massachusetts Bay
Saml. Adams,
John Adams,
Robt. Treat Paine,
Elbridge Gerry.

Rhode Island
Step. Hopkins,
William Ellery.

Connecticut
Roger Sherman,
Sam'el Huntington,
Wm. Williams,
Oliver Wolcott.

New York
Wm. Floyd,
Phil. Livingston,
Frans. Lewis,
Lewis Morris.

New Jersey
Richd. Stockton,

Jno. Witherspoon,
Fras. Hopkinson,
John Hart,
Abra. Clark.

Pennsylvania
Robt. Morris,
Benjamin Rush,
Benja. Franklin,
John Morton,
Geo. Clymer,
Jas. Smith,
Geo. Taylor,
James Wilson,
Geo. Ross.

Delaware
Caesar Rodney,
Geo. Read,
Tho. M'Kean.

Maryland
Samuel Chase,
Wm. Paca,
Thos. Stone,
Charles Carroll of Carrollton.

Virginia
George Wythe,

Richard Henry Lee,
Th. Jefferson,
Benja. Harrison,
Ths. Nelson, Jr.,
Francis Lightfoot Lee,
Carter Braxton.

North Carolina
Wm. Hooper,
Joseph Hewes,
John Penn.

South Carolina
Edward Rutledge,
Thos. Heywood, Junr.,
Thomas Lynch, Junr.,
Arthur Middleton.

Georgia
Button Gwinnett,
Lyman Hall,
Geo. Walton.

NOTES

CHAPTER ONE

1. *The Political Writings of Thomas Jefferson*, ed. Edward Dumbauld (New York: Liberal Arts Press, 1955), p. 8, letter to Henry Lee, 8 May 1825.
2. Alfred North Whitehead, *The Function of Reason* (Boston: Beacon Press, 1958), p. 20.
3. I am indebted to Mr. William Morrisey for reminding me that none of the Declaration's "truths" are self-evident in the Lockean sense. In *An Essay Concerning Human Understanding* (I, ii. 18), only simple ideas, ideas of sensation, are said to be self-evident, e.g., *"White is not black,"* or *"A square is not a circle."* Ideas such as "unalienable rights" are far too complex to be self-evident for Locke. Hence it is misleading to regard the Declaration as a Lockean document. See p. 5 n. above.
4. *The Works of James Wilson*, ed. Robert G. McCloskey, 2 vols. (Cambridge, Mass.: Harvard University Press, 1967), 1: 145-46.
5. *The Living Thoughts of Thomas Jefferson*, ed. John Dewey (Greenwich, Conn.: Fawcett Publications, 1963), pp. 94, 101.
6. Ibid., p. 95.
7. Ibid., p. 191.
8. Hamilton, Madison, and Jay, *The Federalist*, ed. Edward Mead Earle (New York: Modern Library, n.d.), p. 3.
9. *Federalist* 1, pp. 4-5. See also *Federalist* 31, pp. 188-89.
10. See my *Discourse on Statesmanship* (Urbana: University of Illinois Press, 1974), pp. 20-21.
11. *Federalist* 14, p. 85.
12. Ibid.
13. Only to be obscured in another century by commentators preoccupied with the non-rational.
14. It should be noted that I am here contradicting the historically myopic conclusions of "realists" and pluralists who deplore the universalism of American foreign policy, and of course universalism in general, as a major cause of international tension. On this topic, see above, pp. 47-50.
15. Alfred North Whitehead, *Adventures of Ideas* (New York: Macmillan Co., 1933), p. 86.

CHAPTER TWO

1. Alfred North Whitehead, *The Function of Reason* (Boston: Beacon Press, 1958), pp. 37–38. What I have termed the "metaphysical" reason Whitehead calls the speculative reason which, by the way, he associates with Plato in contradistinction to the practical reason which he associates with Ulysses.

2. This is, of course, a theistic position. Nietzsche provides a nontheistic, more precisely, an immanentist doctrine of human dignity. See his *Beyond Good and Evil*, Part IX, "What is Noble? " (Whether Nietzsche's position is politically tenable is questionable.) See also Plato, *Republic*, 377e–383c (on the gods); 514a–517c (on the "Allegory of the Cave"); and 485a–486d (on the qualities of the philosopher).

3. *Function of Reason*, p. 39, where Whitehead is referring to the speculative reason.

4. John Stuart Mill, *Representative Government*, in *Utilitarianism, Liberty, and Representative Government* (New York: E. P. Dutton & Co., 1951), p. 257.

5. Whitehead, *Function of Reason*, p. 26.

6. See Edmund S. Morgan, ed., *Puritan Political Ideas* (Indianapolis: Bobbs-Merrill Co., 1965), p. 257, for the thoughts of John Wise on this subject.

CHAPTER THREE

1. Thomas Hobbes, *Leviathan*, ed. Michael Oakeshott (Oxford: Basil Blackwell, 1955), p. 32.

2. Ibid., pp. 57–60, 37.

3. Ibid., p. 37.

4. Ibid., p. 46.

5. Ibid., p. 104. See *The Works of James Wilson*, ed. Robert G. McClosky, 2 vols. (Cambridge, Mass.: Harvard University Press, 1967), 1: 139. Wilson provides the following admittedly inadequate but nonetheless instructive reply: "It is . . . said, that moral sentiment is different in different countries, in different ages, and under different forms of government . . . ; in a word, that it is as much the effect of custom, fashion, and artifice, as our taste in dress, furniture, and the modes of conversation. Facts and narratives have been assembled and accumulated, to evince the great diversity and even contrariety that subsists concerning moral opinions. And it has been gravely asked, whether

the wild boy, who was caught in the woods of Hanover, would feel a sentiment of disapprobation upon being told of the conduct of a parricide. . . . It may, however, be proper to observe, that it is but candid to consider human nature in her improved, and not in her most rude or depraved forms. 'The good experienced man,' says Aristotle, 'is the last measure of all things.' To ascertain moral principles, we appeal not to the common sense of savages, but of men in their most perfect state.'' With Hobbes primarily in mind, Wilson points out in the sequel that, unlike the ancients, the modern moralists ''give mean interpretation and base motives to the worthiest actions—in short, they endeavor to make no distinction between man and man, or between the species of men and that of brutes.''

6. Karl Marx and Frederick Engels, *The German Ideology* (New York: International Publishers, 1968), p. 14.

7. I tend to agree with those who maintain that Nietzsche, who claimed to be the first true nihilist, overcame nihilism. See Richard Schacht, ''Nietzsche and Nihilism,'' in Robert Solomon, ed., *Nietzsche* (Garden City, N.Y.: Anchor Books, 1973), pp. 58-82. See also the contrary view of Stanley Rosen, *Nihilism* (New Haven: Yale University Press, 1969), chs. 3 and 4, passim.

8. See his dissenting opinion in *Ginzburg* v. *United States*, 33 U.S. 463, 489 (1966). This opinion is, so far as I know, the most blatant example of moral relativism uttered by any public official.

9. Contrary to the wishes and claims of many of its decent adherents, relativism engenders and has aggravated domestic and even international conflict. (1) The New Left turmoil of the 1960's was influenced by an amalgam of three relativistic doctrines, namely, neo-Marxism, neo-Freudianism, and Sartrian existentialism. (2) The increasing number of strikes by public employees and the exorbitant demands and economic blackmail of various interest-groups are symptomatic of an erosion of the notion of the public interest fostered by relativism. (3) The pacifist movement of the 1930's, so largely relativistic in inspiration, sapped the will of the British and French governments and thereby contributed to the ascendency of Hitler and the outbreak of World War II. (4) Finally, both Nazism and Soviet Communism are forms of relativism. See my essay ''Intellectual and Moral Anarchy in American Society,'' *Review of Politics*, 32:1 (Jan. 1970), pp. 36-45.

10. Hobbes, *Leviathan*, pp. 84, 85. Needless to say, Hobbes was not

a pacifist, and pacifism is not entailed by the relativistic moralist, although there is a strong tendency in that direction.

11. Ibid., pp. 46, 64, 104, 438.

12. Here a word from John Adams is instructive: "Does not the increase in knowledge in any man increase his emulation, and the diffusion of knowledge among men multiply rivalries? Has the progress of science, arts, and letters yet discovered that there are no passions in human nature—no ambition, avarice, or desire for fame? Are these passions cooled, diminished, or extinguished? . . . Have these propensities less tendency to divisions, controversies, seditions . . . and civil wars than formerly? On the contrary, the more knowledge is diffused, the more the passions are extended, and the more furious they grow." *The Political Writings of John Adams*, ed. George A. Peek (New York: The Liberal Arts Press, 1954), pp. 189-90.

13. Friedrich Nietzsche, *The Use and Abuse of History* (Indianapolis: Bobbs-Merrill Co., 1957), esp. pp. 28-34, where Nietzsche has primarily in view historicism.

14. Ibid., pp. 28-34.

15. J. William Fulbright, *Old Myths and New Realities* (New York: Vintage Books, 1964), pp. 7, 78, 141. Needless to say, a luxury is anything which is unnecessary for life and health—two values descriptive of Plato's city of pigs. Interestingly enough, Plato's city of pigs was devoid of any "ideology" or abstract notion of justice. It was also devoid of arts and sciences and philosophy, in short, of civilization. This is one reason why it enjoyed a life of health and peace. Another reason is to be found in the absence among its rustic inhabitants of many needs and wants, of avarice and envy, of ambition and pride. Only when their desires multiplied, stimulated, no doubt, by new knowledge, invention, and commerce—in other words, only when they became covetous of wealth or lustful for power—then only did the city of health become sick and subject to war . . . yes, and civilized.

16. J. William Fulbright, *The Arrogance of Power* (New York: Vintage Books, 1966), p. 255. This remark is indicative of the antiphilosophic statesman. It reveals that *The Arrogance of Power* is fundamentally an attack on the "arrogance" of the intellect—that pride of the philosopher who affirms the power of reason to apprehend universally valid truths concerning how man should live.

17. Ibid., p. 162.

18. Contemporary political science sometimes makes a distinction between political theory and political philosophy roughly

corresponding to the "fact-value" dichotomy of logical positivism. The former is regarded as empirical or descriptive, the latter as normative or prescriptive. Accordingly, many so-called political theorists, who deny the possibility of political philosophy (or objective and universally valid knowledge of how men should live), regard their own discipline as eminently practical on grounds that it provides comprehensive and coherent knowledge of how men do in fact live, from which knowledge one may formulate public policies. It should be noted, however, that such policies would be nothing more than the means by which to achieve ends determined by the practicing politician. The political theory in question, therefore, would be morally neutral or value-free.

19. John Stuart Mill, *Representative Government*, in *Utilitarianism, Liberty, and Representative Government* (New York: E. P. Dutton & Co., 1951), pp. 273-75, 284.

20. Fulbright, *Arrogance of Power*, p. 163.

21. Ibid., p. 7.

22. Ibid., pp. 254-55. Compare, however, Henry A. Kissinger, *The Necessity for Choice* (New York: Harper & Row, 1961), p. 45: "In any crisis, rather than show our 'nervousness'—which would be a wise course from the point of view of deterrence—we are much more likely to seek to demonstrate that we are 'calm,' 'rational,' 'calculating,' 'accommodating'—all qualities which, if taken seriously by the aggressor, may cause him to doubt our resolve to resort to all-out war." Did Professor Kissinger anticipate the conduct of Secretary of State Kissinger? Whatever the case, we are entitled to know what has happened since 1960 to alter Dr. Kissinger's understanding of nuclear deterrence; for both the United States and the Soviet Union have now reached the stage of mutual deterrence to which the above statement is addressed. (But see below, p. 119, n. 3.)

23. Fulbright, *Old Myths and New Realities*, pp. 77-78.

24. Hobbes, *Leviathan*, p. 84.

25. "Supplemental Foreign Assistance, Fiscal Year 1966-Vietnam," *Hearings Before the Committee on Foreign Relations*, United States Senate, 89th Cong., 2nd Sess. (Washington, D.C.: U.S. Government Printing Office, 1966), p. 441. Would that General Taylor could have responded to Fulbright as Hamilton did to those who compared the American and French revolutions:

The cause of France is compared with that of America during its late revolution. Would to Heaven that the comparison were just. Would to Heaven that we could discern in the Mirror of

French affairs, the same humanity, the same decorum, the same gravity, the same order, the same dignity, the same solemnity, which distinguished the course of the American Revolution. Clouds & Darkness would not then rest upon the issue as they now do.

I own, I do not like the comparison. When I contemplate the horrid and systematic massacres . . . of September—When I observe that a Marat and a Robbespierre, the notorious prompters of those bloody scenes—sit triumphantly in the Convention . . . —When I see an unfortunate Prince, whose reign was a continued demonstration of the goodness & benevolence of his heart, of his attachment to the people, of whom he was the Monarch—who though educated in the lap of despotism, had given repeated proofs, that he was not the enemy of liberty—brought precipitately and ignominiously to the block,—without any substantial proof of guilt, as yet disclosed—without even an authentic exhibition of motives, in decent regard to the opinions of mankind—When I find the doctrines of Atheism openly advanced in the Convention and heard with loud applauses—When I see the sword of fanaticism extended to force a political creed upon citizens who were invited to submit to the arms of France as the harbingers of Liberty—When I behold the hand of Rapacity outstretched to prostrate and ravish monuments of religious worship erected by those citizens and their ancestors—When I perceive passion, tumult and violence usurping those seats, where reason and cool deliberation ought to preside—

I acknowledge, that I am glad to believe, there is no real resemblance between what was the cause of America & what is the cause of France—that the difference is no less great than that between Liberty & Licentiousness. I regret whatever has a tendency to confound them, and I feel anxious, as an American, that the ebullitions of inconsiderate men may not tend to involve our Reputation in the issue.

The Papers of Alexander Hamilton, ed. Harold C. Syrett, 15 vols., t.d. (New York: Columbia University Press, 1961-69), 14:475-76.

26. "ABM, MIRV, SALT, and the Nuclear Arms Race," *Hearings Before the Subcommittee on Arms Control, International Law and Organization of the Committee on Foreign Relations*, United States Senate, 91st Cong., 2nd sess. (Washington, D.C., U.S. Government Printing Office, 1970), p. 147. In all fairness it should be pointed out that Senator Fulbright regards South

Korea as a dictatorship. But just as relativists obscure the distinction between just and unjust regimes, so they obscure the difference between better and worse dictatorships.

27. Fulbright, *Arrogance of Power*, p. 250.

28. Ibid., pp. 256–57.

29. Alexander Solzhenitsyn, *The Gulag Archipelago* (New York: Harper & Row, 1973), p. 178. See, also, the sequel, *The Gulag Archipelago Two* (New York, Harper & Row, 1975).

30. Solzhenitsyn, *Gulag Archipelago*, p. 161. Earlier (p. 46), Solzhenitsyn relates moral relativism to a loss of pride. As for the extermination figure and the responsibility of Marxist ideology, see his *Letter to the Soviet Leaders* (New York: Harper & Row, 1974), pp. 30, 48.

31. The quoted passage is cited in Richard Pipes, "Some Operational Principles of Soviet Foreign Policy," in Michael Confino & Shimon Shamir, eds., *The U.S.S.R. and the Middle East* (New York: John Wiley & Sons, 1973), p. 7. According to a recent study, the Soviet Union has achieved superiority over the United States in almost every major military category. See "United States / Soviet Military Balance," A Study by the Library of Congress, *Congressional Research Service*, printed for the use of the Senate Committee on Armed Services (Washington, D.C.: U.S. Government Printing Office, 1976), pp. 1–86. Having long been taught to believe that the Soviet Union—sometimes euphemistically called the "other side"—harbors no hostile intentions toward the United States, the American public, Congress included, can hardly be expected to support a strong military defense posture or to counter Soviet expansionism in the Middle East or in Africa.

32. Lyndon Baines Johnson, *The Vantage Point* (New York: Popular Library, 1971), p. 463. It goes without saying that heads of state should not engage in name-calling. But if the American people are not to be lulled into complacency, responsible public officials, including the President, must inform them— *and it is their duty to do so*—about the insidious methods and ultimate intentions of the Soviet Union throughout the world. This may be done without arousing uncontrollable passions. See Charles E. Bohlen, *Witness to History 1929-1969* (New York: W. W. Norton & Co., 1973), p. 345; Dean Rusk, *The Winds of Freedom* (Boston: Beacon Press, 1963), pp. 15, 249, 253, 341, 342, 349; and George F. Kennan, *Memoirs 1925-1950* (Boston: Little, Brown & Co., 1967), pp. 558,

563-64, who, in these works, reject a non-ideological approach to
U.S.-Soviet relations.

33. Rather than say, as certain critics might, that this statement is
so patently false as to place in question whether its authors and
signatories have any abiding respect for truth (or sense of honor),
let us merely observe that it contradicts, almost verbatim, the
following statement made some three years earlier by one of the
foremost authorities on the Soviet Union and a former ambassador
to that country, Charles E. Bohlen: "The classic principles of
Marxism . . . had always been and still are an obstacle to normal
relations between the Soviet Union and other countries. . . ."
The Transformation of American Foreign Policy (New York:
W. W. Norton & Co., 1969), p. 75. In the epilog of his *Witness to
History 1929-1969*, written *after* and with explicit reference to
the SALT I Agreements, Mr. Bohlen warns his readers as follows:
Nearly twenty years after Stalin's death, the political philosophy of the Soviet Union remains virtually unchanged. There
may be some slight theoretical variations, particularly on the
non-inevitability of war. The fact of the matter is that ideology
is just as important to Moscow today as it was in 1934, when I
first stepped on Russian soil. . . .
For the United States, the ideological element of Soviet
policy is of vital importance. It means that there can be no
harmonious relations with Moscow in the customary sense
of the word. . . .
Soviet ideology . . . proscribe[s] adherence to any objective standard of morality. Lies are perfectly acceptable if they
advance the Soviet cause. (This does not mean that the United
States is inherently more moral than the Soviet Union. But we
operate in a society in which good and evil are differentiated;
the Communists do not.) [Pp. 537-38]
And yet, thanks to the teaching of moral relativism, the distinction between good and evil has become increasingly obscured in
the United States; and it is this fact, more than any other, that
will account for the changing relationship between the United
States and the Soviet Union.

34. *Hearings Before the Subcommittee on National Security and
International Operations of the Committee on Government
Operations*, United States Senate, 92nd Cong., 1st sess., Part 4,
March 17, 1971 (Washington, D.C.: U.S. Government Printing
Office, 1971), p. 94. Professor Lewis is a distinguished British
historian.

35. Alfred North Whitehead, *Adventures of Ideas* (New York: Macmillan Co., 1933), p. 63.
36. For an elaboration of this topic, see my *Discourse on Statesmanship* (Urbana: University of Illinois Press, 1974), pp. 154-57.
37. Alfred North Whitehead, *Science and the Modern World* (New York: Free Press, 1967), p. 5.
38. Alfred North Whitehead, *Process and Reality* (New York: Harper Torchbooks, 1960), pp. 76, 79.
39. Whitehead, *Science and the Modern World*, p. 18.

CHAPTER FOUR

1. And indeed logical positivism does not regard moral opinions as *statements* but rather as emotive utterances.
2. The difference between bargaining and compromise is dealt with in my *Discourse on Statesmanship* (Urbana: University of Illinois Press, 1974), pp. 156-57.
3. I fully realize how offensive these words may appear to relativists who parade themselves in the garb of humanism or humanitarianism. Still, there are no *rational* grounds for them to feel indignant with me. I am a man, as worthy of heartfelt concern as the humblest of beggars. Perhaps I will therefore be forgiven for saying that I see in contemporary humanism nothing more than sentimental egalitarianism, quite appropriate for herd-like animals oblivious of what is noble and what is base. Imagine some member of this herd exhorting another to act like a man! Imagine their pledging to each other their lives, their fortunes, *and* their sacred honor!
4. Hamilton, Madison, and Jay, *The Federalist*, ed. Edward Mead Earle (New York: Modern Libary, n.d.), *Federalist* 51, p. 337.
5. Respectively, *Federalist* 10, p. 55, and *Federalist* 37, p. 228.
6. For a critique of pacifism, see *The Collected Essays, Journalism and Letters of George Orwell*, ed. Sonia Orwell and Ian Angus, 4 vols. (New York: Harcourt, Brace & World, 1968), 2: 166-67, 220-30; 3: 374-75.
7. See Hobbes, *Leviathan*, ed. Michael Oakeshott (Oxford: Basil Blackwell, 1955), p. 57, where Hobbes comes very close to contradicting his own atomism by saying "The *value* or WORTH of a man, is as of all other things, his price; that is to say, so much as would be given for the use of his power: and therefore is not absolute; but a thing dependent on the need and judgment of another." Incidentally, in the sequel, Hobbes goes on to say that

"the public worth of a man . . . is that which men commonly call DIGNITY—a position the statesmen of the Declaration would have rejected with contempt, but which position is quite compatible with the democratic psychology prevailing among post-Freudians. In this respect the statesmen of the Declaration were more atomistic than Hobbes, as well as more aristocratic.

8. *Federalist* 31, p. 188.
9. Aristotle, *The Politics of Aristotle*, trans. Ernest Barker (London: Oxford University Press, 1952), p. 316. Needless to say, the cultural relativist precludes himself from making such distinctions.
10. The principle is not an absolute, since it will eventually come into conflict with other moral principles of no less importance. Any moral principle is the product of selective emphasis which obscures the whole on which it is dependent. To absolutize any good would inevitably be destructive of the whole essential for its own enjoyment. All good things, in virtue of their sheer individuality, admit only of finite or limited realization. This means we cannot enjoy all good things undiluted. See Alfred North Whitehead, *Modes of Thought* (New York: Free Press, 1968), p. 51.
11. Alfred North Whitehead, *Science and the Modern World* (New York: Free Press, 1967), pp. 51, 58.
12. *The Political Writings of John Adams*, ed. George A. Peek (New York: Liberal Arts Press, 1954), p. 85.
13. Needless to say I have in mind the Vietnam War, although other distinctions are in order. The American cause in that war was a just and even a noble one. But the manner in which that cause was pursued lacked nobility. I shall have more to say about this subject in *Beyond Détente*.
14. Aristotle, *Politics*, p. 204.
15. See *Federalist* 49, p. 329, where *Publius* refers to experiments in constitutional change as being of "too ticklish a nature to be unnecessarily multiplied."
16. This, so far as it goes, is an application of the Whiteheadian philosophy of organism. It exemplifies what Whitehead has variously called the doctrine of "internal relations" (*Science and the Modern World*, pp. 122-23, 158-65), or of "mutual immanence" (*Adventures of Ideas*, Chs. VIII, XII). Quite clearly Whitehead would reject any atomistic ideas the Declaration may derive from antecedent philosophy, Lockean or otherwise. Only it would be misleading to call the Declaration atomistic. As noted earlier, Jefferson himself suggested that it represents a *political*

synthesis of classical and modern principles. Still, given White-head's notion of universals, the meaning of universal truths, as embodied in the Declaration, would have to be reformulated if they are to be assimilated into his organic philosophy. On the other hand, there may be a middle position implicit in White-head's own understanding of the traditional notion of universals. For if, in the traditional view, "a universal is that which enters into the description of *many* particulars," then the "truth-value" of any universal is a function of its ingression into, or relevance for, every other entity. (See my *Discourse on Statesmanship*, pp. 273-76.)

17. *The Political Writings of Thomas Jefferson*, ed. Edward Dum-bauld (New York: Liberal Arts Press, 1955), p. 187.

18. *Federalist* 14, pp. 84-85, and compare *Federalist* 37, p. 226, *Federalist* 70, p. 457.

19. See Locke's treatment of this section in *The Second Treatise of Civil Government*, secs. 240-42.

20. *The Living Thoughts of Thomas Jefferson*, ed. John Dewey (Greenwich, Conn.: Fawcett Publications, 1963), p. 25.

21. *Political Writings of Jefferson*, pp. 67, 69.

22. Ibid., pp. 49, 69, 98-101.

23. Ibid., p. 91. On the same subject, see also *The Political Writings of John Adams*, pp. 139, 185-86, 203-4.

24. *Political Writings of Jefferson*, p. 38, where, in his *Notes on Virginia*, Jefferson predicted: "From the conclusion of this war we shall be going down hill. It will not then be necessary to resort at every moment to the people for support. They will be forgotten, therefore, and their rights disregarded. They will forget themselves but in the sole faculty of making money, and will never think of uniting to effect a due respect for their rights."

25. See *The Records of the Federal Convention of 1787*, ed. Max Farrand, 4 vols. (New Haven: Yale University Press, 1937), 1: 605.

26. *Thoughts of Jefferson*, p. 125.

CHAPTER FIVE

1. If it is not true that all men are created equal in the sense of being equally subject to the same moral law, then "men" do not constitute a single species, but rather a welter of superior and inferior species, or rather, of individuals, each a law unto himself, in which case tyranny can confront liberty as equally justifiable. This of course recalls the Hobbesian and Lockean state of nature.

In this connection, see John Rawls, *A Theory of Justice* (Cambridge, Mass.: Harvard University Press, 1971), pp. 11–12, 21. Rawls's egalitarian orientation prevents him from squarely facing the consequences of his own equivalent to the state of nature.

2. Even a New England town-hall democracy had to appoint officials to conduct affairs and had therefore to give them some discretionary power.

3. On this point, see *The Political Writings of Thomas Jefferson*, ed. Edward Dumbauld (New York: Liberal Arts Press, 1955), pp. 60, 90.

4. Ibid., p. 75.

5. *The Works of James Wilson*, ed. Robert G. McClosky, 2 vols. (Cambridge, Mass.: Harvard University Press, 1967), 2:788.

6. John Stuart Mill, *Representative Government*, in *Utilitarianism, Liberty, and Representative Government* (New York: E. P. Dutton & Co., 1951), p. 378.

7. See my *Discourse on Statesmanship* (Urbana: University of Illinois Press, 1974), pp. 196–99, for an elaboration of this topic.

8. Of course, the qualifications for privileges must not be so high as to make a mockery of the principle of equality of rights.

9. The full text of this document will be found in Theodore McNelly, ed., *Sources in Modern East Asian History and Politics* (New York: Appleton-Century-Crofts, 1967), pp. 329–31. Consistently with its exclusion of the word "honor," the document "repeal[ed] all the international obligations that France had so far subscribed to on behalf of Vietnam." Here Ho Chi Minh merely followed the Bolsheviks who, in 1918, repudiated the international obligations of the Kerensky as well as the Tsarist regime.

10. The notion that all *peoples* are equal and have a right to be happy corresponds to the notion that all racial or ethnic groups composing a single society are equal; that the members of each group are entitled to the various benefits and privileges of society, not on the basis of individual merit, but merely on the basis of group affiliation. It would be as if each group comprised a distinct species of beings, each self-enclosed and self-justified. Accordingly, no overarching standard of excellence would be recognized or have any efficacy in the relations between these groups, a standard by which to determine whether a member of one group was superior or inferior to members of another group. Lacking such a standard—it might be merely the notion of the *common* good—a member of one group could claim the right to enjoy any benefit

or privilege enjoyed by members of any other group, and without regard to his personal qualifications or individual merit, but again only on the basis of his group affiliation (and the group's size relative to the population of the whole society). By claiming the right to enjoy the goods of society without regard to merit or desert, the individual is in effect claiming a right to be happy in contradistinction to the right to pursue happiness.

11. Cited as Andrew Johnson, *Speeches* (Frank Moore, ed., Boston, 1965), 56, in Carl Russell Fish, *The Rise of the Common Man 1830-1850* (New York: Macmillan Co., 1946), pp. 10-11. In this connection it is well to quote at length from Lincoln's Springfield speech of June 26, 1857. There he points out that while the authors of the Declaration of Independence "intended to include *all* men [in the phrase "all men are created equal"] . . . they did not intend to declare all men equal *in all respects*. They did not mean to say all were equal in color, size, intellect, and moral developments, or social capacity. They defined with tolerable distinctness, in what respects they did consider all men created equal—equal in 'certain inalienable rights, among which are life, liberty, and the pursuit of happiness.' This they said, and this they meant. They did not mean to assert the obvious untruth, that all were actually enjoying that equality, nor yet, that they were about to confer it immediately upon them. In fact they had no power to confer such a boon. They meant simply to declare the *right*, so that the *enforcement* of it might follow as fast as circumstances should permit. They meant to set up a standard maxim for free society, which should be familiar to all, and revered by all; constantly looked to, constantly labored for, and even though never perfectly attained, constantly approximated, and thereby constantly spreading and deepening its influence, and augmenting the happiness and value of life to all people of all colors everywhere." See *The Collected Works of Abraham Lincoln*, 9 vols. (New Brunswick, N.J.: Rutgers University Press, 1953-55), 2:405-6.

12. See Alfred North Whitehead, *Religion in the Making* (Cleveland: Meridian Books, 1961), p. 94.

13. This conforms to James Wilson's thoughts on the subject, only Wilson uses the terms liberty and freedom synonymously: "The name liberty we give to that power of the mind, by which it modifies, regulates, suspends, continues, or alters its deliberations and actions. By this faculty, we have some degree of command over ourselves: by this faculty we become capable of conforming

to a rule: possessed of this faculty, we are accountable for our conduct." *Works of James Wilson*, 1: 211. See also Hamilton, Madison, and Jay, *The Federalist*, ed. Edward Mead Earle (New York: Modern Library, n.d.), *Federalist* 53, pp. 347–48, where Madison speaks of "rational liberty," and Edmund S. Morgan, ed., *Puritan Political Ideas* (Indianapolis: Bobbs-Merrill Co., 1965), pp. 138–39, 256–57, for the thoughts of John Winthrop and John Wise on the same subject.

14. B. F. Skinner, the noted behaviorist, recently wrote a book entitled *Beyond Freedom and Dignity*. Though Skinner's teaching is one-sided and pernicious, one can still appreciate his intellectual courage, his attempt to spell out the linguistic, moral, and social implications of his behaviorism. Most behaviorists prefer eclecticism which, though more sober, is intellectually indolent.

15. Alfred North Whitehead, *The Function of Reason* (Boston: Beacon Press, 1958), p. 16.

16. Even the meaning of what constitutes life has become politically controversial in recent years. The development of organ transplants and substitutes will greatly complicate the matter in the near future.

17. Alfred North Whitehead, *Science and the Modern World* (New York: Free Press, 1967), pp. 49, 58, 91.

18. Even if there were one outstanding individual who possessed more wisdom and virtue than the collective wisdom and virtue of the representative body, still it would be unwise to endow him with complete power if only because he could not ensure an equally wise and virtuous successor. But see Plato, *Republic*, 546 a–e; *Politics of Aristotle*, trans. Ernest Baker (London: Oxford University Press, 1952), pp. 150–52; Mill, *Representative Government*, pp. 271–72.

19. Unfortunately, "group-interest" theorists have minimized the importance of forms. See, for example, Bertram Gross, *The Legislative Struggle: A Study in Social Combat* (New York: McGraw-Hill Book Co., 1953), ch. 1.

20. Interestingly, Jefferson opposed such a tenure.

21. See my *Discourse on Statesmanship*, p. 437.

22. See Alfred North Whitehead, *Adventures of Ideas* (New York: Macmillan Co., 1933), p. 99: "It is a false dichotomy to think of Nature *and* Man. Mankind is that factor *in* Nature which exhibits in its most intense form the plasticity of nature."

23. See John Stuart Mill, *On Liberty*, p. 203, but compare pp. 157–58, 161–62, and *Representative Government*, pp. 238–41, 256–58, 286, 296.

24. Relativists do not quite grasp the significance of this seemingly paradoxical principle. If I may recur to an earlier theme, relativists believe that the practice of self-determination merely requires international tolerance, the mutual toleration of the inevitable differences among nations. They consciously or unconsciously assume, however, that such differences are in fact reconcilable. Recall Senator Fulbright: "Are we to regard the communist countries as more or less normal states . . . with whom we can never [be] reconcile[d]?" But the truth is that it is not possible to reconcile a tolerant democracy to an intolerant tyranny, especially a tyranny which has never renounced its long range objective of world dominion. As Lincoln might have said, this world cannot remain permanently half slave and half free. Sooner or later it must become all one or the other. I shall have more to say about this very issue in the sequel to the present work. To avoid misunderstanding, however, I should here point out the United States is not under any moral obligation to rid the world of servitude. Of course, if we regard communism of the Marxist-Leninist variety as evil, then, like any other evil, we should in some tangible and *publicly recognizable way* be committed to its *ultimate* extinction. Meantime, the policy of containing that evil would seem to be the dictate of prudence. With Senator Fulbright we certainly want to "conserve" the world from nuclear destruction. The only question is whether the Senator's relativism really serves that end, or whether, instead, it will so undermine the moral fiber and self-determination of free men as to lead, eventually, to universal servitude.

25. In this connection, see *Federalist* 49, p. 329.

26. *On Liberty*, p. 96. See also *Representative Government*, p. 259, where Mill prescribes the form of government most conducive to the cultivation of intelligence and virtue. Despite the disclaimer (ibid., p. 306), the form which Mill calls "representative government" is in truth a "mixed regime" of aristocratic proportions.

27. See my *Discourse on Statesmanship*, p. 276.

28. See *The Political Writings of John Adams*, ed. George A. Peek (New York: Liberal Arts Press, 1954), p. 34, where Adams writes: "The simple forms of government are monarchy, aristocracy, and democracy. . . . A government formed upon these three principles in due proportion is the best calculated to answer the ends of government and to endure." See also my *Philosophy of the American Constitution* (New York: Free Press, 1968), Ch. 9, on the Presidency, especially pp. 167-69, 190-91.

Library of Congress Cataloging in Publication Data

Eidelberg, Paul.
    On the silence of the Declaration of independence.

    Includes bibliographical references
    1. United States. Declaration of independence.
I. Title.
JK128.E35   320.5'0973   76-8759
ISBN 0-87023-216-9